CW00421034

THE HISTORY OF WALLSEND BOYS' CLUB

AUTHORS

Vince Carrick, Michael McGill and Margaret Scott

First published in the United Kingdom in 2013 by Potts Print (UK) Limited, NE23 1WG

ISBN 978-0-9927712-0-1

Foreword:

In October 2003 Wallsend Boys' Club held a special event to mark the retirement of three long-serving officials; David Beardall, who had been Club Leader since the 1965 rebuilding of the club, Joe Kirtley who had been Club President since 1976, and Robert Slone, voluntary football coach for over 35 years.

This event, alongside the fact that the 40th anniversary of the 'new' club was approaching, prompted two members of the club committee, Vince Carrick and Michael McGill, to start investigating the club's history with a view to producing a commemorative booklet.

In researching for their heritage project they found that there was more than enough material for a book, recorded mainly over the years in newspaper cuttings and magazine articles. Inevitably much of this related to the outstanding football success of the club since 1965. But they were surprised to find that the club's earlier history was also able to be recorded, mainly through the reminiscences of a remarkable group of 'Old Boys', some of whom had been founder members in 1938 when the first Wallsend Boys' Club was started. This group, including Ray "Pang" Oliver, Jack Carruthers, Jimmy McBlain, Bill Watson, Jack Scott, Fred "Spud" Tate, Eddie "Bunty" Young, Norman Livingstone, Tony Corkhill and John McNally, were able to breathe life into the early stories of the first club. As Michael commented during the drafting of this history, the fact that the club were able to bring together some of this group of 'Old Boys' was one of the unexpected bonuses of the whole heritage project.

A further fascinating development was the discovery that there had been an earlier Boys' Club in Wallsend, whose history stretched back a century to 1904. What particularly linked this early club with the official WBC, was the strong connection which both had with the management and workers of Swan Hunter's shipyard. This 'Swan connection' is a story in its own right.

This version of the Club history ends at 2005 when that 40th anniversary was celebrated. Sadly, the most recent headlines about the club are of the demise of the 1965 clubhouse and, as a result of this, a temporary curtailing of much of the non-footballing activity of the club. I have no doubt however that this will be a temporary situation. Wallsend Boys' Club has gone through difficult and dramatic times before and has managed to rise like the phoenix which was its emblem for so long.

This history simply tells the story so far from the turn of the century to 2005 – a century of remarkable development. I have no doubt that in times to come it will be updated to recall some of the highlights of the later decades of the 21st century .

Margaret Scott

September 2013

AUTHORS

Vince Carrick

Michael McGill

Margaret Scott

Contents

In a number of picture captions throughout this book 'TBC' has had to be used when no name was available. If you are that person please contact us so we can include your name in future reprints.

Full contact details can be found on our website www.wallsendboysclub.org.uk

Wallsend Boys' Club

Presidents

Sheriton Clements Swan ....1938 – 1969

Jimmy McBlain...................................1969 – 1976

Joe Kirtley ....1976 – 2003

Peter Kirkley......................................2003 – to present day

Leaders

Ernest (Sandy) Laws ....1938 – 1952

Allan (Skipper) Ruse ....1952 – 1958

Frank Herdman ....1958 – 1959

David Beardall....................................1965 – 2003

Brian Nicholson ....1967 (Caretaker Leader)

Garry Marshall ....2003 – 2010

Dawn Convery....................................2011 – Present Day

Other Boys' Club Staff (The early years)

Woodwork Instructor:..........................J. Haldon ....(1938 – 1950)

Assistant Club Leader: ....L. Gallon ....(1938 – 1948)

Boxing Instructor: ....L. Teasdale................................(1938 – 1942)

Assistant leader:.................................R. Oliver....................................(1939 – 1954)

Assistant Leader:................................T. Fairbridge.............................(1939 – 1954)

Assistant Leader:................................W. Ogilvie.................................(1940 – 1946)

Wrestling Instructor: ....S. Pouton ....(1940 – 1942)

Club Cleaner:.....................................Mrs Dodds ....(1940 – 1944)

Assistant Leader:................................E. Smith ....(1944 – 1950)

Club Cleaner:.....................................Mrs Nichols...............................(1944 – 1950)

Assistant Leader:................................R. Smith ....(1944 – 1948)

Wardrobe Mistress (pantomime)..........Mrs Thain ....(1948 – 1952)

Woodwork Instructor:..........................A. Thompson ....(1948 – 1950)

Football Trainer: ....B. Mason...................................(1949 – 1952)

Pro-Wrestler and Army Cadets: ....J. Smith

Assistant Leader:................................S. Briggs

Club Committee: ....Mr Riseborough

Club Committee: ....G. Swaddle

Club Committee: ....I. McFarlane

Founder and Early Members 1938 – 1950

Ronnie Adams ....Football

Dennis Allen.......................................Boxer

Colin Allison ....Football, music, cubs

Eddie Appleby ....Won amateur cup with Crook town
and was also a gymnast

Tom Appleby ....Football, sprinter and gymnast

N. Armstrong ....Pantomime

Eddie Ashcroft...................................Football

D. Balbrirnie.....................................Pantomime

H. Bell ....Pantomime

Henry Bird..Pantomime (tap dancer)

Ernie Boult ....Wrestling

John Bracken.....................................Football

Ted Briggs ....Assistant leader

Ronnie Buckham ....All-rounder

H. Brownlee ....Pantomime

Harry Byers.......................................All-rounder

Andy Campbell..................................Football and pantomime

Jim Cant...Pantomime and boxing

Jack Carruthers ....Pantomime

Len Cassie ....All-rounder

George Charlton.................................Pantomime and Army cadets

Hugh Cockburn ....Pantomime and Army cadets

Ted Cockerill.....................................Army cadets

L. Collins ....Pantomime

Ernie Conway ....All-rounder

K. Conway ....Football

Bob Dixon...Football

Bert Dobinson ....All-rounder

H. Dobinson ....Pantomime

Walter Dodds.....................................Football

Vince Donnelly ....Football

S. Edwards ....Pantomime

Tom Fairbridge ....Assistant leader

V. Finlay...Pantomime

Kevin Flannery ....Football

S. Fothergill.......................................Pantomime

K. Fraser ....All-rounder

Fred Galloway ....Electrician for the pantomimes

George Gardner ....Football

Jackie Gardner ....Football and pantomime

Richard Gibbons ....Football and pantomime

T. Green ....Accompanist (pantomime)

Len Grey ....All-rounder

John Hiffle ....Football

Les Hiftle ....Football

Walter Howeth ....Football and pantomime

George Hunham ....All-rounder

Jonny Ingham ....Professional footballer

Arthur Irving ....Boxer

P. Jones ....Pantomime

Bill Jordan ....Football

Tom Kirtley ....All-rounder

George Lake ....All-rounder

Ron Lane ....Pantomime

John Leeson ....Boxer

Syd Leeson ....Boxer

Tom Leeson ....Boxer

J. Lindsay ....Pantomime

Bill Lowes ....Boxer

Ivor Martin ....All-rounder

Ken Martin ....All-rounder

Bob Mason ....Football trainer

L. Massey ....Pantomime

Jack Matthews ....Football

Jimmy McBlain ....Became President 1969

R. McCarthy ....Pantomime

P. McClean ....Pantomime

J. McFarlane ....Pantomime

John Moran ....Football and singer

P. Mullen ....Pantomime

K. Murphy ....Pantomime

Mel Murphy ....Football and pantomime

F. Nichols ....Pantomime

Ron Nichols ....Boxer, gymnast and pantomime

Danny O'Fee ....Football

Ray Oliver ....Gymnast, football manager and pantomime

Stan Oliver ....All-rounder

M. Pennie...Pantomime

Tom Potts ....Football

J. Poulter ....Pantomime

Dave Redhead ....Boxer and football

C. Richardson ....Pantomime

Doug Richardson ....Football

Bill Rigby...Boxer

H. Riley ....Pantomime

Tom Ripley ....Army cadets

Jim Robson..Electrician for pantomime

Norman Rudd ....Music (Panama Jazz Band)

Jim Samson.......................................Football

Jack Scott ....Woodwork and pantomime

Les Scullion ....Football

'Tut' Singleton...................................Boxer

L. Sloan ....Pantomime

Bob Snell ....Football and pantomime

Fred Spall ....All-rounder

Eric Stapyleton ....All-rounder

Jack Stubbs ....Football

George Swaddle ....Football

Jimmy Swan......................................Football and pantomime

Fred 'Spud' Tate ....Pantomime and army cadets

Jack Taylor ....Football

Norman Thain ....All-rounder

Alfie Thompson ....All-rounder

K. Train ....Pantomime

R. Turnbull ....Pantomime

J. Wake..Pantomime

Milton 'Minga' Wallis ....Pantomime

Tom Wedderburn...............................Football

George Wells ....Boxer

L. White...Pantomime

Jackie Whitehouse.............................All-rounder

George Wilson ...................................C.S.M. army cadets and boxer

Eddie Young ....Football

John Young..Football

Willie Young ....Football

Chapter 1 - The Birth of Wallsend Boys' Club – The 'L' shaped 'wooden hut'

The official history of Wallsend Boys' Club starts in the years of the Great Depression in Wallsend. Like many areas of the country, Wallsend had rough times in the twenty years after World War I ended. The 1920s had seen the slow collapse of old industries like coal mining and shipbuilding, and of course there had been industrial unrest with the General Strike taking place in 1926.

Things had got worse after the Crash of 1931, and by 1933 nearly four out of five shipbuilding workers were unemployed. This hit towns like Wallsend, where so many were dependent on shipbuilding, very hard. As an indication of the scale of the crisis, in 1931 Swan Hunter made profits of £150,000. By 1933 their profits were down to £19,000.

This situation wasn't unique to Wallsend of course, so in the mid-1930s the government started to identify areas where they feared high unemployment rates were having an adverse effect on young men, with the intention of supporting the building of boys' clubs to provide a focus for the young.

Wallsend was one of the places to benefit from this scheme. The idea was that if local benefactors would contribute, the cost of the actual labour would be covered by a grant from the government to the local Ministry of Labour Department who would supervise the project.

The upshot of these circumstances was that in 1938 building began on a plot of land on Station Road to the north of the centre of Wallsend. The land in question was next to the High Farm Residents Association hut, just opposite the end of Prince Road, and had been used by them to erect a large marquee for their annual flower and vegetable show.

What was being built there in 1938 was an 'L' shaped 'wooden hut' which was to be the home of the official Wallsend Boys' Club, affiliated to the National Association of Boys' Clubs. Jack Scott, one of the founder members has been able to provide a sketch of the building as seen below.

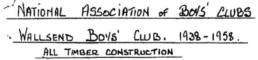

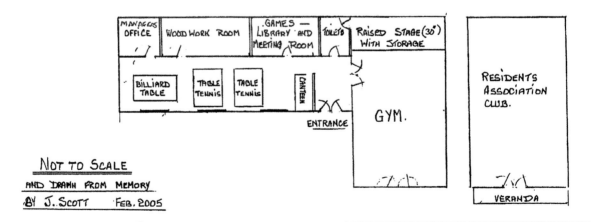

WALLSEND BOYS' CLUB.

STATION ROAD,
WALLSEND-on-TYNE.

APPLICATION FOR GRANT TOWARDS THE COST OF BUILDING

AND EQUIPING THE ABOVE.

M A T E R I A L S.

JOINERY.	58. 9. 0.	
TIMBER.	324. 4. 10.	
FOUNDATIONS.	85. 17. 0.	
ROOFING.	127. 0. 0.	
GUTTERING.	17. 17. 8.	
DRAININGS.	15. 12. 4.	
GENERAL SANITATION.	20. 16. 0.	
WATER.	10. 0. 0.	
STEELWORK. by Contract including erecting.	160. 0. 0.	
HEATING.	120. 0. 0.	
PAINT, PUTTY, and GLASS.	30. 0. 0.	
IRONMONGERY.	19. 1. 3.	
LIGHTING.	26. 0. 0.	
TOOLS.	10. 0. 0.	
SUNDRIES.	30. 0. 0.	
TEMPORARY FENCING.	15. 0. 0.	
HAULAGE. etc.	6. 0. 0.	1075. 18. 1.

MEALS AND CLOTHING FOR MEN.	£100. 0. 0.	
BOOTS AND OVERALLS FOR MEN.	13. 12. 0.	113. 12. 0.

GYMNASTIC APPARATUS contd.

ONE. GYMNASTIC SPRING-BOARD, ash cross-piece and blocks.	2. 16. 0.	
THREE. best quality FIBRE MATS @ £2.10.0. each.	7. 10. 0.	
ONE. Gymnastic Mattress. 12' x 4' x 2½".	4. 4. 0.	
6 DOZEN. GYMNASTIC VESTS @ 18/- doz.	5. 8. 0.	
6 DOZEN. GYMNASTIC SHORTS @18/- doz.	5. 8. 0.	
6 DOZEN. GYMNASTIC SHOES @ 18/- doz.	5. 8. 0.	
6 DOZEN. TOWELS @ 12/- dozen.	3. 12. 0.	
2 sets. BOXING GLOVES @ 22/- set.	2. 2. 0.	
2 Ceiling to floor punch balls with gloves. £1. 11. 3d. ea.	3. 2. 6.	48. 0. 6.

FOOTBALL EQUIPMENT.

TWO. DOZEN. FOOTBALL JERSEYS @ 32/6d.	3. 5. 0.	
TWO. DOZEN. Prs.FOOTBALL STOCKINGS. @ 22/6d.doz.	2. 3. 0.	
TWO. DOZEN.prs. FOOTBALL SHORTS. @ 18/6. doz.	1. 17. 0.	
TWO. GOALKEEPERS. SWEATERS @ 8/6d.	17. 0.	
FOUR. FOOTBALLS.	2. 10. 0.	10. 12. 0.

WOODWORK AND HANDICRAFT EQUIPMENT.

6 BENCHES. 4'6" x 2' complete with vices. @ £2. 7. 6d. each.	12. 15. 0.	
3 Nail Punches.	9.	
6 - 2ft rules.	12. 0.	
3 sets. Chisels. ¼" to 1¾".	1. 6. 3.	
3 Sand-paper blocks.	9.	
3 Sets of bits.	14. 3.	
3 Padsaws.	3. 9.	
6 Marking Gauges.	6. 0.	
3 Bradawls.	1. 0.	
2 Iron Jack Planes.	1. 17. 0.	
3 Iron Smoothing Planes.	1. 19. 6d.	
3 Spokeshaves.	3. 0d.	
6 squares	6. 0d.	
6 Panel Saws.	16. 6.	
1 Hatchet.	3. 6.	
3 pinchers.	3. 0.	
2 Sets of Screwdrivers.	10. 0.	
1 Oil stone.	1. 9.	
Carried forward.	22. 0. 0.	£1,248. 2. 7.

Copy of documents from 1938 outlining the cost of the building & equipment.

Ironically, by the time the wooden hut was being built in 1938, the worst of the Depression was over for Wallsend, with the shipyards filling up again due to the rearmament programme which was gathering pace. Nevertheless, there was still unemployment, and the firm of Swan Hunter were happy to be the main benefactor of the club. Their support was personified by one of the Directors, and grandson of the founder of the firm, Sheriton C. Swan. Wallsend Council had donated the plot of land to the Boys' Club for a peppercorn rent. All the materials were provided from the shipyard, which also supplied skilled workers where necessary to finish off the building work. Reed Milligan, the glass company, also contributed labour and finance. The bulk of the actual labour on the building came from the unemployed however, who were paid through the government grant with meals and clothing.

Within a couple of months of starting, the building was up and ready, and very quickly being used for a whole range of activities. In total it had cost £1297.10s.0d to build and equip, with £113.12s.0d of that going to feed and clothe the unemployed labourers.

On April 13th 1939, some months after opening its doors to members, the club was officially launched. The ceremony was carried out by the Duchess of Northumberland in the presence of local dignitaries and guests. Mr Sheriton Clements Swan, president of the club, presided over the large gathering. He was supported by Mrs S. C. Swan, Mr & Mrs C. S. Swan, Lord Ravensworth, Sir Cecil & Lady Cochrane, Mr P. Denham Christie, Mr N. M. Hunter, Mr W. G. Pearson (Chairman of the club), and Mr Brand, Canon & Mrs Hurst, Mr J. W. L. Adams, the Mayor of Wallsend and Town Clerk, Members of the Town Council, President of the Wallsend Rotary Club, Mr Young, and others.

WALLSEND BOYS' CLUB.

Approved Estimate Feb. 1938

	£. S. d.	£. s. d.
Building materials	822.10. 0.	
Water, sanitation and Drainage.	46. 8. 0.	
Heating.	120. 0. 0.	
Lighting	26. 0. 0.	
Fencing	15. 0. 0.	
Tools	10. 0. 0.	
Haulage and sundries	36. 0. 0.	1075.18. 0.
P.T. and recreation equipment	63.12. 0.	
Handicraft equipment	31. 7. 0.	
Office and canteen equipment	13. 1. 0.	108. 0. 0.
Meals and clothing for unemployed men working on the scheme		113.12. 0.
		£ 1297.10. 0.

In his introduction to the president, Mr Pearson said that he was sure that he would not just be a president in name because the association of the firm with the club was a very real one. This was certainly true. Not only had Swan's been instrumental in the setting up of that 1938 club, they had also been involved in a forerunner since the turn of the century as the next chapter illustrates.

On that opening night in 1939, Sheriton C. Swan spoke of his pleasure in being invited to be the first president. He pointed out that 80% of the members at that time were apprentices at Swan's and so welcomed the maintenance of close contact with the club. Like everyone else that night he paid tribute to the work of the unemployed men who had built the club. He is quoted in the Wallsend Herald as saying:

"I wish to record the splendid action of the unemployed men who gave their labour voluntarily and built this magnificent building. This, I think, shows a commendable spirit, worthy of a special mention, and I would like them to know how much their action is appreciated, not only by the organisers, but also by us all, including the boys themselves.

My earnest wish is that the boys of Wallsend will make full use of the facilities provided here, and I am confident that not only will they thoroughly enjoy the various activities now, but they will in the future benefit from their early associations with the club."

Mr Swan then welcomed the Duchess to the platform to perform the official opening ceremony. She herself said, "I hope the boys who use this Club will always remember the men who built it for their benefit. I am glad to hear that many of them have now found employment. To all I say: thank you for your great work for the young generation."

Lord Ravensworth and Mr Young also spoke. Canon Hurst emphasised the help that the unemployed men, members of the Wallsend Social Services Centre, had given in building the club, and pointed out that the Tyneside Council of Social Service had backed the scheme from its inception.

The Mayor, in his speech, revealed that the Wallsend Corporation had given the site, and he wished the boys and the Club every success.

Mr Teasdale, secretary of the Northumberland Association of Boys' Clubs, also spoke and Mr Sandy Laws, newly appointed club leader, thanked those who had given assistance and gifts to the Club.

The evening closed with the singing of the National Anthem.

Ernest (Sandy) Laws
Wallsend Boys' Club Leader 1938.

Neither the Duchess, nor any of the people present, could have dreamed that the club they had just opened would still be going strong into the 21st century, and that over a hundred years after Swan's great triumph, the Mauretania, being launched in 1906 it would be looking confidently to the future and planning for future 'young generations'.

Wallsend Boys' Club's first logo.

Chapter 2 – The Swan Hunter Connection: The corrugated iron hut

Several references have already been made to the strong links between the firm of Swan Hunter and Wallsend Boys' Club. It's worth putting some of the history of the Swan family into this account to illustrate the strength of those connections. It can be seen from this chapter also that Swan's already had a history of involvement with a Boys' Club in Wallsend before the 1938 club came into being.

In 1853 Charles Mitchell (originally from Aberdeen) opened the Low Walker Shipyard and in the following year married Anne Swan, the daughter of a farmer at Walker, at the new Walker parish church.

In 1873 Charles Mitchell also took over the running of the Wallsend shipyard. The following year his brother-in-law Charles Sheriton Swan was appointed senior manager at the yard. The resulting business became known as C. S. Swan and Company, with C.S. Swan making the business a resounding success. Tragedy struck the family in 1879 when Charles Sheriton Swan was killed in the English Channel while travelling home from Russia on a business trip with his wife Mary. He fell from the bows of a paddle steamer, suffering fatal injuries.

George Burton Hunter, a ship builder from Sunderland became the new Swan's Managing Director, in partnership with Charles Sheriton Swan's widow, Mary. In 1880 the firm was therefore re-named C. S. Swan and Hunter. Mary's son, Charles Sheriton Swan Jnr, became a director of the firm at the age of 25 in 1895.

Charles Sheriton Swan junior, son of Swan's founder, who became a director of C.S. Swan and Hunter at the age of 25 and was knighted for his services to shipbuilding during the Second World War.

In 1883 George Burton Hunter built the 'Wallsend Café' on the south west corner of the junction of Station Road and the High Street. [1] His purpose in providing this facility was to encourage his twin interests in temperance and education. There were two sections to the Wallsend Café. One was devoted to meals and refreshments, with rooms for Clubs, Trade Union meetings, and other community purposes. And the other, the "Athenaeum" was devoted to education and recreation. According to Richardson's "History of the Parish of Wallsend", by 1887 Wallsend Café had about 300 regular students who took classes in a range of technical subjects including 'steam, theoretical and

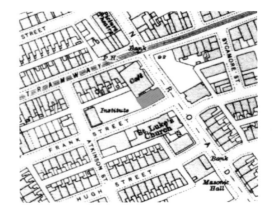

Map showing location of Wallsend Café and corrugated hut.

applied mechanics', naval architecture, and mathematics and languages. Young apprentices from the shipyard were particularly encouraged to use these educational facilities.

[1] Details in Richardson's History of the Parish of Wallsend.

By the turn of the century this commitment to the welfare of the apprentices had taken another turn, with a Boys' Club being opened officially on November 14th 1904. The club had two rooms which were situated in the main Café building, one for reading and one for games. In addition to this, they seem to have had a gymnasium situated at the rear of the Café. According to the Wallsend Herald, which covered the opening, this was well equipped with bars, rings, vaulting horse and ladders. The boys also had access to a corrugated iron building which had been erected on land just south of the Café in 1904. Primarily, the building was to be used by Mr. J. F. Doughty and his fellow missioners in Wallsend, including the vicar of St Luke's church, Reverend William Marlow O'Brady-Jones. But it was also, according to the 'Wallsend Herald' of December 1903, to be used by the Boys' Club which had just been started.

Rev William Marlow O'Brady-Jones.

At the official opening Mr Hunter spoke of his anxiety to give all the apprentices at the shipyard every chance of progressing and becoming good citizens. This theme was continued in an address given by Mr De Russet, a director of the firm. He spoke of the immense advantages to be enjoyed by present day apprentices compared to a generation earlier, and urged the boys to take every opportunity to attend evening classes at the club in order to better themselves. He particularly warned them about the dangers of drinking, playing cards, or gambling. The Wallsend Herald quotes him as saying that he had started out with none of the opportunities they had, yet here he was, naval architect with the firm building the largest ship in the world. His words weren't idle boasting, since the Mauretania was at that time being built at Wallsend by Swan Hunter and Wigham Richardson.

> The Wallsend Cafe Company are about to utilise the piece of railed in ground lying to the south of their premises by erecting a commodious corrugated iron building, which is to be used as a meeting place by Mr J. W F. Doughty and those associated with him in his mission work in Wallsend. Mr Doughty has, during the few years he has resided in our midst done great service in the cause of religion amongst a class of people whom the Church and other denominations had a difficulty in reaching. The building will also be used by the Boy's Club, an organisation which has been set on foot at the Wallsend shipyards and which is intended to embrace practically all the apprentices employed there. I shall have something further to say on the question of the Boy's Club in subsequent issues of the " Herald."

Wallsend Herald 24th December 1903.

By the time the Mauretania was launched in 1906 it would seem that the club had developed its interests towards football also. In October of that year Wallsend Old Boys A.F.C. formed, with Rev. O'Brady-Jones being the first president. The club was based in the corrugated hut, but obtained the use of a field on the road to the Isolation Hospital (now the site of Wallsend ambulance station at Kings Vale) for matches at a rent of 30/- per season. The club's rules were drawn up as follows:

1. The club shall be called "The Wallsend Old Boys A. F. C."
2. Club colours, white shirts with blue knickers.
3. The selection committee to consist of Team Captain, President, Vice Captain, Secretary and two other members.
4. The selection committee to meet every Sunday night at 8.45pm.
5. Members unable to play to let the Secretary or Captain know before Thursday morning.
6. Subscriptions 2/- per annum. Half to be paid by December 1st. Fixture cards free to members.
   A balance sheet to be published at the end of the season.

Clearly this earlier club had very strong connections with the firm of Swan Hunter and the official Wallsend Boys' Club seems to be its natural successor. One main difference was the fact that it was part of the National Association of Boys' Clubs set up in 1925.

The N.A.B.C. had been formed, not to be the centre of a new movement however, but to link together a number of existing bodies and clubs.[2] One of these existing bodies was presumably the club for apprentices that had been formed in 1904.

By the 1930s, just before the opening of Wallsend Boys' Club, when the Depression was at its worst, Charles Sheriton Jnr, kept men employed at the yard by setting them to work making garden furniture because he did not want the work force to disband. He and his wife Gertrude had four children, one son and three daughters.

Their son Sheriton Clements Swan came into the business as he had already qualified as an ordinary architect rather than a naval architect and with his wife Rosalind, designed interiors for several ships. He eventually became a director of Swan Hunter and it was he who was instrumental in setting up and running Wallsend Boys' Club, becoming the Club's first President in 1938. The vast majority of the Boys' Club members in 1938 were employees of Swan Hunter.

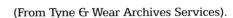
(From Tyne & Wear Archives Services).

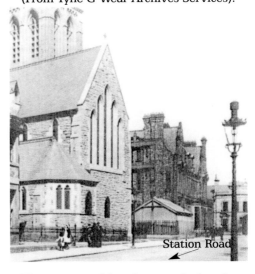
Station Road

The corrugated iron hut attached to the Wallsend Café 1904.

Corrugated Hut

St. Lukes Station Road.

[2] Principles and Aims of the Boys' club movement published in 1930.

Apart from Mr Swan himself, other members of the firm were supporters of the club. Mr Pearson, the personnel manager at Swan Hunter was on the Boys' Club committee for many years according to Jack Carruthers, a founder member. (See next chapter for more from Jack and other founder members). Jack recalls that Mr Pearson would help club members to obtain apprenticeships at Swan Hunter's. Jimmy McBlain recalls that the inaugural committee of the club also included Vic Stevens, company secretary at Swan Hunters, and Joe Jackson, who was a time clerk there.

Sheriton Swan held his position as President, for over 30 years, throughout the club's life in the timber building on Station Road, and also in the new building, which was opened in 1965 up until 1969 when he resigned from that position for personal reasons. His place as President was taken by one of the original club members from 1938, Jimmy McBlain.

In the early days of the Boys' Club Sheriton would grow fruit and vegetables in his back garden and then take the produce down to the shipyard and sell them to the employees, and the proceeds were donated to Wallsend Boys' Club. Swan Hunter donated money and labour to help with the up-keep and maintenance of the building for many years as seen from a covenant signed in May 1952.

The donations of £100 given by S.H. & W.R., and Wallsend Slipway to Wallsend Boys' Club are allowed for tax purposes. Therefore the cost to each Company (Allowing for Income Tax & Profits Tax Relief) is only £50. A covenant at the figure of £50 would only realise £95.5.0. (Tax at 9/6d.), instead of £100 we are now getting. There is no means whereby we can get more from these donations without involving additional cost to the respective Companies.

"If each Company were prepared to give a covenant for £75 per annum, this donation to the Club would amount to £140 p.a. x 2 = £280. An increase of £80 p.a. to the Club at a cost of £25 p.a. to each Company."

When the 1965 building was designed, included in the plans were a central staircase and first floor walkway designed specifically to look like a ships bridge. Also in 1965 a new Club logo was designed, incorporating a swan in the centre. This was produced as a mark of appreciation to Sheriton Clements Swan for his outstanding contribution to the Boys' Club over many years. The Boys' Club used the Swan logo for over thirty-five years.

Wallsend Boys' Club logo 1965.

Sheriton and his wife Rosalind had a son David, who in 1968 joined Swan's as a Quality Control Engineer.

David was the fourth generation of "Swans" in the company.

Sheriton Clements Swan died in 1986.

David Swan, great grandson
of Swan's founder.

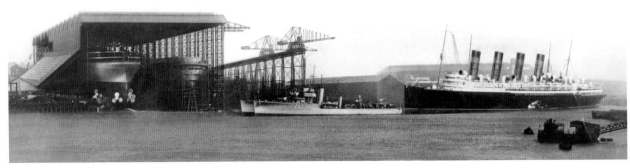

Chapter 3 - Early years and founder members: 1938-1945:

The war time club

Although Wallsend Boys' Club is now associated so strongly with football, it is clear that the club begun in 1938 had a very wide range of activities. These took place under the leadership of Ernest "Sandy" Laws who was club leader from 1938 to 1952. As recalled by Jack Carruthers, Sandy was about 40 years old when he started managing the club in 1938. And lived on Benton Road in Newcastle. (According to Jack, Sandy "smoked like there was no tomorrow". He was apparently called "Sandy" because he resembled the nationally known comedian Sandy Powell.) Founder member Jimmy McBlain recalls that in 1938 subscription fees for the new Wallsend Boys' Club was 1d (one old penny).

Ernest (Sandy) Laws.

No sooner had the opening ceremony taken place, the national context changed from one of Depression to preparation for war. From March 1939 war had begun to seem likely and the rearmament programme escalated and air raid shelters were built. When war eventually came in September 1939 the Boys' club continued to meet, undoubtedly providing some much needed light relief for those involved with it, although inevitably being touched with tragedy at times when members became war casualties. During the war years there was an air raid shelter situated behind the residents' hall, which was to the right of the Boys' club. Whenever the siren went off, the Boys' club members and staff would file into the air raid shelter, where invariably club member Ronnie "Pick" Nichol would start off a sing song to help keep every ones mind off what was going on outside.

John McNally.

According to John McNally's essay the club building was taken over by the Ministry of Defence during those years and used for fire watching.

In spite of this, the club's activities continued and were very varied. They can probably best be described through the reminiscences of those who were among the first members.

Wallsend Boys' Club Boxing Team 1941.
Back Row: Ronnie Lawson, George Wilson, George Charlton, Jack Carruthers, Ronnie Dunbavin, Tommy Leeson, George Wells, John Leeson Bill Watson.
Middle Row: Billy Lake, Joe Huntington, Ernie Watson, Bill Rigby, Dave Redhead, Eric Schofield.
Sitting: Sid Leeson, Ron Nichol, Ronnie Buckham. On Seats: Ernest (Sandy) Laws (left)
Laurence (Skipper) Teasdale (right).

Jack "Major" Carruthers (pictured fourth from left back row) was one of the founder members, joining the club in 1938, and he remembers being active in the club's first football and boxing teams. The boxers were coached by Laurence "Skipper" Teasdale and by Joe Bird, the father of Henry Bird whose story is told later. In the early years of the club the boxing ring was marked out on the floor, but as boxing grew in stature a proper raised ring was often borrowed from Vaux Breweries of Sunderland.

"Golden Gloves" competitions were held at the Ritz Cinema on Wallsend High Street to help raise funds for the Boys' Club. The event would be held over a period of six days, with one bout held each day immediately before the film show. Jack Carruthers recalls fighting in the first night bout in 1940. Inter-youth competitions were also held at St James' Hall in Newcastle, with Wallsend Boys' Club and Grainger Park Boys' Club the top teams in the competition. On Wednesday January 21st 1942 Wallsend Boys' Club hosted the preliminary Northumberland County Boxing Tournament, with the admission prices being 1/6 for non-members with club members being admitted for half price.

Bill Watson was another founder member from 1938 whose main activity at the club was boxing. He recalls Skipper Teasdale as being a top boxing coach who coached at other clubs as well as Wallsend, including All Saints Youth Club based under Byker Bridge and Willington Quay Boys' club. He also ran the boxing club at Grainger Park in Newcastle, which is still a centre for boxing on Tyneside. Joe Bird was never slow in coming forward with a little bit of additional advice for his young boxers with some "tricks of the trade" thrown in for good measure. At one bout at the Boys' club, Bill fought Tommy Leeson, Tommy thrashing Bill, "nearly knocking him into next week". Bill came away with a somewhat "enlarged" face, split lip and a bruised body. Bill went away vowing to have a re-match with Tommy and this time he intended to give a better account of himself. After spending a couple of weeks recovering and allowing the swelling to go down, Bill who did not possess a pair of boxing gloves himself, borrowed a pair from an ex professional boxer who gave him some advice and Bill went off for some intense training down beside the burn in Wallsend. Bill stayed away from the Boys' club while he continued his training and when he felt ready he arranged for a re-match between himself and Tommy at the Boys' club. Tommy had no idea that Bill had been training away from the Boys' club and when the bout started Bill used all his new skills to help him to defeat Tommy. "A very satisfactory night's work".

According to Bill, Tommy, and his two brothers, John and Sid, were very good boxers. Apparently Tommy was also the only boxer who could afford a gum shield at the time. On Monday April 29th 1940, Bill fought in the Amateur Boxing Championships held at the new St James' Hall in Newcastle in aid of the Journal and Evening Chronicle War Fund and Boys' clubs. Entry for spectators cost 6d.

In 1936 Bill Watson had been a goalkeeper with his main sport being football. Not being used to kicking the ball from the turf, one day Bill kicked the ground instead of the ball, breaking his foot. When he went to see the doctor / bone setter he was told to take up boxing as dancing on his toes would help him regain the full use of his foot. This is how he re-directed himself into taking up a new amateur career in boxing. Bill recalls Sandy Laws as an outstanding Boys' Club Leader who "gave his all" in the development of young people.

One of the boxers at the Boys' club, George Wells, later turned professional. George fought Stan Hawthorn who later fought for the British title. Another club member who turned professional was heavyweight Dave Redhead, whom every boy at the club tried to avoid boxing because of his "killer" punch. Dave had two professional fights in Glasgow, where he unfortunately found out that he also had a "glass chin" and was knocked out in both contests. This marked the end of Dave's professional career.

Not all boxing memories from the era were of victories. Eddie Young, who joined the club at the age of 16 in 1944, remembers a night at St James' Hall in Newcastle when a club member, Wayne Cresswell, had to fight a huge lad from the Grainger Park club. Eddie's memory is that as his opponent joined him in the ring, Wayne took one look and decided that discretion was the better part of valour, making a hasty retreat back to Wallsend.

Apart from boxing, in 1941 wrestling was introduced to the club when professional wrestler "Dirty" Jack Smith, from St James' Hall, came once a week to train the members in unarmed combat.

Football was also a popular activity at the club during those years. Jimmy McBlain recalls that there were three eleven-a-side teams. Football strips were purchased or donated to the club by various organisations. Johnny Ingham, who became a professional player with Gateshead, played for Wallsend Boys' Club team from 1941 – 1942. He was a "one-club man", sticking with Gateshead when several top First Division clubs like Newcastle United, Sheffield United and Huddersfield Town courted his services. He was rated the best outside right in the old Third Division north and starred in the Gateshead side that reached the quarter-finals of the Cup in 1953, beating Liverpool along the way. Johnny Ingham scored both goals at Bradford and netted again at Hull to help Gateshead into the sixth round when they played Bolton Wanderers at Redheugh Park. Bolton won through a Nat Lofthouse goal and went on to Wembley.

Joe Harvey, who skippered Newcastle at the time, always reckoned that United should have signed Ingham and Tommy Callender. Johnny Ingham was one of the first to link the name of Wallsend Boys' Club with quality footballers. When he died in May 2000 he was described as epitomising all that was good about that era of football. Eddie (Bunty) Young also recalls a very good club team led by Tommy McCarther. They played in the Boys' Club League until they were 16 and then formed an Old Boys' team and played in the newly formed South East Northumberland League before then moving to the Northern Amateur League. Another member of the club during those years was Raymond "Pang" Oliver, who managed to join at the age of 13 when the minimum age was really 14. Ray's big interest at the club was gymnastics, at which he excelled. During the 1930s and 1940s cinemas were hugely popular, with no less than five cinemas in Wallsend.

Ray (Pang) Oliver demonstrating his gymnastic skills at Wallsend Boys' Club 1950.

Note: The white letters on wall, were used as row numbers when pantomimes were held at the Boys' Club.

There were always queues which would often run the length of the cinema, and buskers would sometimes perform to the waiting queue. Ray (all five foot four of him) would join the lines of people in the queue with his mates from the Boys' club and would perform gymnastic stunts on the pavement along the length of the queue to entertain those waiting.

Fred (Spud) Tate, who joined the club in 1941, describes Ray Oliver, and Eddie and Tom Appleby, as being exceptional gymnasts. Eddie was also an excellent footballer who played for Crook Town in the Amateur Cup Final, whilst Tom became a professional sprinter. Gymnastics took place in the main hall of the club, which became the auditorium when shows or pantomimes were held.

Constitution of Wallsend Boys' Club

CONSTITUTION
of the
WALLSEND BOYS' CLUB.

NAME.

1. The Club shall be called the Wallsend Boys' Club (hereinafter referred to as "The Club").

AREA.

2. The Area of the Club shall be Wallsend.

OBJECTS.

3. The objects of the Club shall be to promote the mental physical and social welfare and education in its widest and most liberal interpretation, of boys normally resident in this area, most of whom would on the grounds of expenses, otherwise be denied the advantages which are sought to be conferred upon them by the object aforesaid.

MEMBERSHIP.

4. (a) Membership of the Club shall be open to all boys who are between the ages of 13 and 18 years, who are resident in the district and who shall comply with the rules and bye-laws of the Club.

GENERAL MEETINGS.

5. (a) An Annual General Meeting of honorary members shall be held each year in MAY for the purpose of receiving an annual report and statement of accounts; to elect honorary officers, and to appoint a Boys' Club Committee.

(b) Further general meetings shall be held at such times as the Boys' Club Committee may decide.

(c) At least 14 days' notice shall be given of any general meeting.

MANAGEMENT.

6. (a) The Club shall be managed by a Boys' Club Committee (hereinafter referred to as the Club Committee) of a minimum number of six members, who shall be elected at the Annual General Meeting of the honorary members.

(b) The Club Committee shall be empowered to co-opt up to a maximum of five members.

(c) The members of the Club Committee shall be honorary members of the Club.

POWERS OF CLUB COMMITTEE.

7. (a) The Club Committee shall elect its own Chairman and Vice-Chairman out of its own number. At all meetings the Chairman shall be entitled to vote and shall also have a second or casting vote.

(b) The Club Committee may form any sub-committees that may be necessary to carry out the work of the Club, may delegate any of its powers to any such sub-committee, and may add to such sub-committee any members who are not members of the Club Committee.

(c) Five members shall form a quorum.

(d) The Club Committee shall have power to make any appointments that may be necessary for the management of the Club.

(e) The Club Committee shall have power to make all bye-laws that are necessary for the management of the Club.

(f) The Management Committee shall have power to borrow money as they deem necessary from time to time for the purposes of the Club.

OFFICERS.

8. (a) The Honorary Officers of the Club shall be the President, a Chairman, Treasurer and Secretary. These, with the exception of the President shall be elected at the Annual General Meeting.

(b) The officers shall be ex-officio members of the Club.

CLUB LEADER.

9. (a) The Club Committee shall appoint a Leader for the Club.

(b) In the event of a Club Leader not being a paid official of the Club, he shall be considered as one of the officers.

PROPERTY AND TRUSTEES.

10. (a) There shall not be more than four Trustees of the Club. The first Trustees shall be:-

W.G. PEARSON, ESQ., C.B.E., J.P.

H. BRAND, ESQ.

S.C. SWAN, ESQ.

H. HUNTER, ESQ.

(b) These Trustees shall hold office until death or resignation, and in the event of such death or resignation, the vacancy thereby caused shall be filled by a General Meeting.

(c) The Trustees shall deal with the property of the Club as directed by the Club Committee (of which an entry in the Minute Book shall be conclusive evidence) and they shall be indemnified against risk and expense out of the property of the Club.

- 3 -

FINANCE.

11. (a) The ordinary finances of the Club shall be raised by donations, members' subscriptions, and proceeds of special efforts. The minimum subscriptions for members shall be as the Club Committee shall direct, but no change in the amount shall be made without the approval of the majority of the members at a general meeting.

(b) The financial year shall terminate on 31st March of each year.

(c) The Club shall not be liable for any expenditure that has not been sanctioned by the Club Committee, or by any sub-committee to which the power of authorising such expenditure has been delegated.

(d) All cheques on the ordinary funds of the Club shall be signed by any two of the following: Chairman of the Club Committee, Hon. Treasurer, or the Hon. Secretary.

(e) The accounts of the Club shall be audited each year in the month of May by a qualified accountant.

(f) Organisers of special efforts on behalf of the Club funds, and sections of the Club which shall organise subsidiary activities involving financial receipts, payments or commitments, shall submit audited statements covering their particular efforts and activities, when called upon to do so.

ALTERATION OF CONSTITUTION.

12. No alteration of this constitution shall be made except at a general meeting of the Club. Notice of any proposed alterations shall be given in writing to the Club Secretary, at least 21 days before each meeting and a copy of the notice inserted in the circular calling that meeting.

The above is the Constitution of the Wallsend Boys' Club, as adopted at a General Meeting, dated 20th September, 1941.

W.G. PEARSON   Chairman.

E. LAWS   Secretary.

Dated 24th September, 1941.

(as amended at an Annual General Meeting held on 14th December, 1944).

For Fred Tate (left) and Jack Scott (right), one of the main attractions at the Boys' Club was the very active craft and woodworking section. This was led by John Haldon, who at the time taught woodwork at St Peter's Church of England School in Wallsend. (He later taught at Kings' School in Tynemouth).

Both Fred and Jack recall the very high standards that their instructor insisted upon with Jack also recalling Mr Haldon as a 'real gentleman'. All woodwork projects were made with 'proper' joints and assembled without the use of pins or glue. Only hand tools were used and with these very complex items were made, such as radiogram cabinets, bedside cabinets, ironing boards, stepladders, and writing bureaus. John Haldon taught the boys one evening a week, and during the other evenings they worked on their projects in the craft room. During the war year's timber was of course in short supply, so the boys acquired old furniture (including pianos) and stripped down the wood to recycle it. Often the wood acquired in this way was of very high quality like rosewood, walnut and mahogany. The finished items would be waxed or French polished, but never painted. When new materials were used, the boys had to pay for them. After completion the best items were often put into the NABC Handicrafts competitions. These competitions were open to all youth organisations throughout Northumberland and

also to the youths held at remand centres throughout the county. Jack Scott won three First Class Award of Merit Certificates from the County Association, one in April 1951 for a bedside cabinet and two more in April 1952 for a smoker's stand and a radiogram cabinet. After competitions the boys could take the articles home. Some of these items of furniture are still being used today, over sixty years later.

Fred was also an active member of the club's football team and as he got older he was invited to join the selection committee. Both Fred and Jack were also members of the Army Cadet Corps. Jack left the club in 1952 and Fred in 1946.

The Boys' Club possessed an old wind up gramophone to play 78 rpm records. Eventually the needle was worn out and as the needles were like gold dust the members used a fine nail. This worked, but considerably shortened the life of the records. However, there was clearly a great tradition in the club of making their own entertainment apart from sporting activities, since the reputation of the club for excellent pantomimes and other shows seems to have grown from year to year.

The first pantomime produced and performed at the club was "Robin Hood" in December 1939. As with the subsequent shows, Sandy Laws was the writer, producer, and director, and also played a leading role, invariably the Dame. About 30 of the members took part in that first show, and of course, all the female roles were played by boys! A tradition going back to Shakespeare's time! Approximately thirty boys were in the cast.

Pantomime Robin Hood at Wallsend Boys' Club 1939.

It would appear that the pantomimes became an, almost, annual event, each December or January, with records remaining of 11 up to 1950. They included Cinderella in 1941, Babes in the Wood in 1942, Robinson Crusoe in 1943, Jack and the Beanstalk in 1944, and Little Red Riding Hood in 1945.

In the years just after the war ended they continued until 1950, with Dick Whittington in 1949 and, finally, Mother Goose.

As photographs and newspaper reviews demonstrate, these were very professional affairs and they played to full houses every night for a week. (The auditorium held about 200 people in the audience according to Jack Scott.) Fred Tate remembers Jack Carruthers as being one of the star turns. (He was Maid Marion in the 1939 show.) Jack could tap dance and was a natural comedian. Tom Kirtley often took the role of the leading man, and was an

Ray Oliver in Pantomime.

excellent singer. Fred himself took part in the shows, and other regulars included Jimmy McBlain, Jimmy Swan, George Charlton, Hughie Cockburn and "Minger" Wallace, Joe Dyce and Ronnie (Pick) Nichols. Eddie Young recalls Pick as being a very talented all rounder at sport as well as being an accomplished ballroom dancer (trained at the Hammill School of Dancing) and a pianist. According to Fred Tate two young musically inclined members later went on to play professionally, Norman Rudd joining the famous "Panama Jazz Men" and Colin Allison playing piano in the social clubs.

Apart from performing in the shows, club members helped out in a variety of back stage capacities. Jimmy Robson, who was employed by Swan Hunter, did the lighting for some of the shows. Ray Oliver was the stage manager for some shows, and Tommy Fairbridge was responsible for the scenery and also sometimes acted as House Manager during the performance week. Photographs of the various shows illustrate how professional the

Stage hands. John Haldon rear left Eddie Young 3rd from left. Front John Hiftle, Ray Oliver, Albert Hood.

costumes were. Sandy Laws had connections with the Palace Theatre in the Haymarket in Newcastle, and with the Grand Theatre in Byker, and sometimes costumes were borrowed from them.

Ray Oliver recalls more intricate costumes being hired from a theatrical supplier in London and delivered in wicker baskets.

To save on expenses Sandy would hire the costumes for three days and "accidentally" send them back two days late. The costumes for Red Riding Hood in January 1945 came from W. Mutril Ltd in Edinburgh. Extra chairs for the shows would be borrowed from the Memorial Hall.

In the second pantomime, Cinderella, which was performed in 1941, the part of Buttons was taken by a young RAF volunteer reservist called Henry Bird. Henry's father, Joe, was heavily involved in the Boys' Club as a boxing coach (as referred to earlier) and had also been a foreman riveter working on the construction of the Tyne Bridge. According to Jack Carruthers, Joe had fitted the first and last rivets on the bridge and when it was officially opened by King George V in 1928 he was in the presentation party and shook hands with the king.

Jack Carruthers says that it was Henry Bird who taught him to tap dance. Apart from this, Henry excelled at art, and he attended art classes at Kings College, Newcastle, (later to become Newcastle University) and was also a member of the Boys' Club at the same time. He was a keen sportsman, playing football, cricket, and tennis and was a keen amateur boxer.

On the main wall at right angles to the counter in the Boys' Club canteen was a painting of a woodland scene done by Henry. It was one of his early attempts at oil painting and appeared to be one of those "Paintings by numbers" pictures. The picture was of beams of autumn sunlight filtering through the woodland trees. It is almost certain that it didn't survive when the building was gutted by fire in 1959.

Alan Heward, who, as a young boy, was a neighbour of the Bird family, retold Henry's story for the local press years later. According to this account, Henry had joined the R. A. F. Volunteer Reserve unknown to his mother, (possibly before he was eighteen), and it was about this time that he had been rehearsing for the Christmas Pantomime in which he played the part of "Buttons". Henry had a blue bellboy uniform similar to that which Bruce Forsyth wore early in his stage career as "Boy Blue". In his role as "Buttons" Henry befriends Cinderella and is a shoulder for "Her" to cry on.

Henry was at No. 4. Gunnery School at Morpeth at the time, and rushing back to Wallsend for rehearsals in his off-duty time.

Henry as an Air Cadet with his Mother.

Christmas came, and he turned up at the Boys' Club on stage in full flying gear, ready for a quick change into his pantomime costume. The pantomime was a great success.

Soon afterwards, Henry was called up properly and became a member of a pathfinder squadron based in Cambridgeshire.

According to the official Bomber Command losses for the 20/21st October 1943 Sgt. Henry James Bird was the rear air-gunner in the Lancaster Bomber MKIII JA701, OL-E, of 83 Squadron, 8 Pathfinder Group based at R. A. F. Wyton, Cambridgeshire.

The aircraft took off from the airfield at 17-47 hours on an operation to Leipzig and was lost without trace. All seven members of the crew including Sgt. Bird were presumed to have been killed in action and are commemorated on the Runnymede Memorial.

This was the first operation on such a distant target at the very limit of their range. Fuel was limited to a minimum because of the heavy bomb load, and many Lancaster Bombers failed to make it back. Many crashed in the North Sea. The weather conditions were appalling and there was rain with thunder and lightning over Leipzig that night making it impossible to find the target. It may well be that Henry Bird's aircraft got hopelessly lost and ran out of fuel, or perhaps it was shot down by hostile enemy aircraft, or hit by German anti-aircraft gunfire. Walter R. Thompson states in his book "Lancaster to Berlin" that on that night two aircraft from 83 Squadron were forced to abort, and two more aircraft were shot up by enemy aircraft.

Henry Bird was only 20 years old at the time of his death. He lived at 80, Exeter Road, Sunholme Estate, Wallsend.

Some of the cast of Cinderella recall that as Jack Carruthers came on stage in the title role, (attempting to look as feminine as possible), one bright spark in the audience shouted: "You look more like Mae West than Cinderella!"

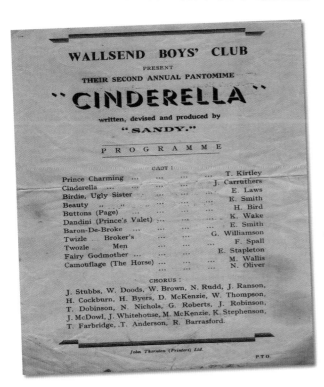

Jack Carruthers as Cinderella
in Pantomime Cinderella at Wallsend
Boys' Club 1941.

In that same year of 1941 Teddy Briggs became assistant manager of Wallsend Boys' Club.

The cast of Babes in the Wood 1942.

In 1942, Wallsend Boys' Club performed their third Annual Pantomime "Babes In The Wood" and again this was a sell out.

The Boys' Club produced its fourth pantomime in 1943, "Robinson Crusoe" again in the club premises. They were well booked up for a week's run including a Saturday matinee, and hoped to raise £50 for club funds. Jack Carruthers reckons that a "small amount" of the funds raised went to the "charitable" cause of purchasing a new suit for Sandy Laws.

Forty members of the clubs 250 were in the show, in which they played all the roles, principals and chorus, and some of them made remarkably "good" girls. The scenario was as in the past performances, by Sandy Laws, and the scenery was homemade and hand painted.

The performance revealed a good deal of talent among the principal actors, particularly the comedy trio of Geoff Wilson, "Capt Skull", Jack Carruthers, "The mate", and Hughie Cockburn, "The boson". Tom Kirtley played the title role,

Jack Scott as Miss Polly and Tommy Kirtley as Robbie in Robinson Crusoe 1943.

Jack Scott was "Polly Perkins" (Principal "Girl"), Ernest "Sandy" Laws was the "Dame", Milton Wallace was "Man Friday" and others notable were Fred Spall "Simple Sammy", Ronnie Nichols, a nice boy singer, "Willie Crusoe", and Kenneth Wake as the "Emperor". The pianist was Mrs A. L. Anderson.

In 1944 Wallsend Boys' Club presented its fifth annual pantomime "Jack and the Beanstalk". Written and produced by Ernest "Sandy" Laws.

Stage Director: L. Gallon
Stage Manager: R. Oliver
Stage Electrician: J. Robson
Pianist: H. Cordes

During this pantomime Hugh Cockburn played the part of Giant Blunderbore on stilts. Each night at the end of the show one of the chorus would push Hugh (still on his stilts) back, and, as he fell, a member of the cast would catch him, saving him from smashing to the floor.

On the last night of the pantomime the cast member who should have caught Hugh mysteriously went AWOL at the crucial time and poor Hugh crashed down on the floor, stilts and all, greatly amusing the audience but giving Hugh's back a real battering. A little bit of skulduggery appeared to have taken place.

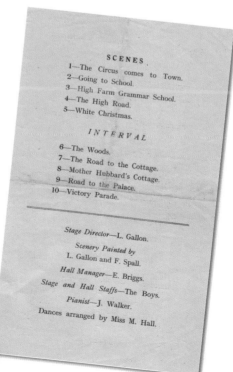

PROGRAMME.

WALLSEND BOYS' CLUB

PRESENT

THEIR FIFTH ANNUAL PANTOMIME

"Jack and the Beanstalk"

WRITTEN, STAGED AND PRODUCED BY
ERNEST LAWS.

Cast in order of appearance.

Immortals—FAIRY GOODWILL ... ... R. Nichols
HUMBUG (GIANT'S SLAVE) ... G. Allison
Mortals—TISH ⎫ KING'S ... J. Carruthers
TOSH ⎭ HENCHMEN ... A. Humpress
KING ... ... G. Charlton
PRINCESS CRYSTAL ... ... F. Tate
JACK ... ... T. Kirtley
MOTHER GRUMPET ... ... E. Laws
SIMPLE SIMON ... ... F. Spall
MINNIE (THE COW) ... { R. Oliver
{ B. Dobinson
GIANT BLUNDERBORE ... H. Cockburn

CHORUS.

"Ladies"—J. Hughes, C. Adamson, H. Knox, N. Douglass, K. Johnson, E. Adamson, T. Farbridge, K. Venus, J. Murphy, W. Cuthbertson, W. Venus, J. Linsdell.

Gents.—T. White, R. Snell, W. Harrison, J. Gibson, J. Middleton, J. Gardner, T. Rooney, T. Appleby, B. Linsdell, J. McBlain, A. Hughes, L. Russell.

1945 saw Wallsend Boys' Club present its Sixth Annual Pantomime, "Red Riding Hood" written, staged and produced by "Sandy".

Six Spectacular Scenes, including ten hit songs and Costumes by W. Mutril, Ltd, Edinburgh. (Over 100 Costumes).

Evening performances started at 7.15pm and admission prices were 2/6, 1/6, 1/0. The show ran for one week.

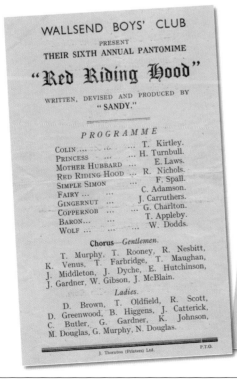

WALLSEND BOYS' CLUB

PRESENT

THEIR SIXTH ANNUAL PANTOMIME

"Red Riding Hood"

WRITTEN, DEVISED AND PRODUCED BY
"SANDY."

PROGRAMME

COLIN ... ... T. Kirtley.
PRINCESS ... ... H. Turnbull.
MOTHER HUBBARD ... E. Laws.
RED RIDING HOOD ... R. Nichols.
SIMPLE SIMON ... ... F. Spall.
FAIRY ... ... C. Adamson.
GINGERNUT ... ... J. Carruthers.
COPPERNOB ... ... G. Charlton.
BARON ... ... T. Appleby.
WOLF ... ... W. Dodds.

Chorus—*Gentlemen.*

T. Murphy, T. Rooney, R. Nesbitt, K. Venus, T. Farbridge, T. Maughan, J. Middleton, J. Dyche, E. Hutchinson, J. Gardner, W. Gibson, J. McBlain.

Ladies.

D. Brown, T. Oldfield, R. Scott, D. Greenwood, B. Higgens, J. Catterick, C. Butler, G. Gardner, K. Johnson, M. Douglas, G. Murphy, N. Douglas.

J. Thornton (Printers) Ltd.   P.T.O.

SCENES.

1—The Circus comes to Town.
2—Going to School.
3—High Farm Grammar School.
4—The High Road.
5—White Christmas.

INTERVAL

6—The Woods.
7—The Road to the Cottage.
8—Mother Hubbard's Cottage.
9—Road to the Palace.
10—Victory Parade.

Stage Director—L. Gallon.

Scenery Painted by
L. Gallon and F. Spall.

Hall Manager—E. Briggs.

Stage and Hall Staffs—The Boys.

Pianist—J. Walker.

Dances arranged by Miss M. Hall.

WALLSEND BOYS' CLUB,

STATION ROAD, WALLSEND,

Present their Sixth Annual Pantomime:

RED RIDING HOOD

Written, Staged and Produced by "SANDY,"

In Six Spectacular Scenes. — Ten Song Hits.

Costumes by W. Mutril, Ltd., Edinburgh. (Over 100 Costumes).

Commencing

MONDAY, JANUARY 1st, to SATURDAY, JAN. 6th, 1945.

FOR ONE WEEK ONLY.

Evenings 7-15 p.m.   Saturday Matinee 2-30 p.m.

Evenings 2/6, 1/6, 1/-.   ,,   ,,   2/-, 1/-

All Seats Booked Free.   BOOK NOW.

Scenes You Will Remember : "The Circus Patrol,"
"High Farm Grammar School," "Ice Ballet," "Victory Parade."

REMEMBER "ALL THE GIRLS" ARE "BOYS."

John Thornton (Printers) Ltd.

Apart from the pantomimes, there were other drama activities taking place in the boys' club. In March 1942 the final of the NABC Drama tournament was held at the Wallsend club, with the home team winning the senior section with a performance of "The Postmasters of Ispahan". The junior team came second with "The Maker of Dreams". In the same year Wallsend Boys' club performed "Salute the Soldier", with Jack Carruthers, Hughie Cockburn, and Tommy Green starring. This production was repeated in 1943.

Jack Carruthers and Hughie Cockburn in Salute the Soldier at Wallsend Boys' Club 1942.

Jack Carruthers in Salute the Sailor at Wallsend Boys' Club 1943.

Jack Carruthers, Ron Nichol and Hughie Cockburn in pantomime at Wallsend Boys' Club 1943.

BBC radio 'Children's Hour', locally based at New Bridge Street, Newcastle, (opposite the Oxford Gallery nightclub), produced plays, using youths as actors. Three members of Wallsend Boys' Club were invited to take part in three of the Children's Hour plays, with Fred Tate (the keen wood worker) being one of the three budding stars. The first production was entitled "Hadrian's Wall" and was broadcast from the Newcastle studio on 16th September 1944. Fred was paid the handsome sum of one guinea (one pound, one shilling) for taking part in the play. If Fred was asked to do a repeat performance he was paid 5/3d. (Five shillings and three pence). A second production entitled "A Modern Bobby Shaftoe" was due to be broadcast on 28th November 1944 but was cancelled at short notice. The third production to

Fred Tate.

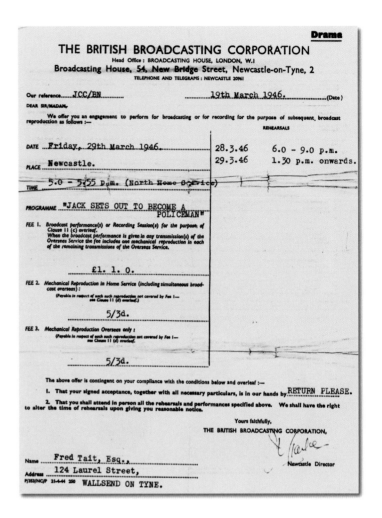

go out on air with Fred in the cast was "Jack Sets Out To Be A Policeman" which was broadcast on 29th March 1946. Due to some misinformation from Sandy the club leader, Fred missed the third production. The BBC were kind enough to pay Fred his guinea, as he was not at fault. The BBC at a later date in January 1948, wrote to Fred asking him to attend auditions for "The Stars Look Down" but Fred declined the offer, this being the end of his career in radio broadcasting. Fred eventually left Wallsend Boys' Club in 1946. During the war years there was an Army Cadet Corps based at the Boys' Club run by Sergeant Major George Wilson. (This later moved to the Vine Street Drill Hall.) To encourage the boys to 'knuckle down', he would give some of his junior soldiers "rankings" within the Cadet Corps. Jack was elevated to the three stripes of a sergeant. One weekend the Cadet Corps sent a group of members to the rifle rage at Ponteland which was run by full time army staff. Jack was among the lads sent there and on arrival all the juniors had to stand on parade to meet the commanding officer. The officer asked jack why he was wearing three stripes on his arm and Jack explained about the cadets being promoted at the Boys' club cadet corps. The officer laughed and for the rest of the weekend Jack was called the 'novice sergeant'.

Camping trips with the Boys' club were not solely connected with the Army Cadet Corps. Bill Watson recalls that Mr Grossman, who owned a shop selling model railways on Croft Street in Newcastle, was a great benefactor of the club. He financed two day camping trips to Hawick Hall in Northumberland. The boys travelled there in a bus provided by Mr Grossman and then camped in bell tents in the hall grounds. There would be activities such as 'tug-of-war', and in the evenings Cecil McCormack would play his harmonica around the camp fire and there would be a sing-song. (Cecil McCormack later went on to become a professional footballer, playing for Middlesbrough and Notts County.)

There were also regular summer camps during the school holidays for those who could afford to go. In June 1943 there was a camp at Wark and in 1944 a summer camp at Rothbury. The boys would be joined at these camps by their own leaders, including Sandy Laws, and by boys from other clubs in Northumberland or Durham. Mr Edward Roberts, the organising secretary of the NABC attended these camps, and his wife was usually the chief cook (and the only female present).

Whilst at Rothbury the Club formed a 'scratch' football team to play against the local village team. Wallsend Boys' Club team won 18-0 and the local team refused to ever play against the Boys' club again.

When the Boys' club football team played against an army team at Wark camp, Jack

Wark Camp 1943 Arthur (titch) Irving and Fred Tate wearing boxing gloves.

Cook House Rothbury 1944
George Swaddle, TBC, George Lake, Jack Scott, TBC, Fred Tate, TBC, Stan Johnson.

Carruthers broke his leg in the game. Also at the Wark camp, Sandy Laws, along with John Haldon and Eric Smith helped stage shows with Wallsend Boys' Club members at the village

Rothbury Camp 1944
Tom Wedderburn, George Waddle, Leslie Blacket, TBC, Mr Roberts, TBC,TBC,TBC,TBC,TBC,TBC, Tony Blackwell, TBC, George Lake, Jack Scott, TBC Fred Tate, George Swaddle, TBC

hall. Another club member, Jim Sampson, who was big and strong, was taught by coaches at Wark to throw the javelin. He proved so good at this that at a competition in the camp against the coaches Jim threw the javelin more than twice the distance of the experts.

It can be seen by the range of these activities that the club took seriously the purpose adopted in its constitution, which was not actually adopted until 1941. In it, the object of the club is stated as being to "promote the mental, physical and social welfare and education in its widest and most liberal interpretation, of boys normally resident in this area, most of whom would on the grounds of expense otherwise be denied the advantages which are sought to be conferred upon them by the object aforesaid".

In 1942 Justin Evans who was Secretary for Training for the NABC wrote an article called, "The Work of a Full Time Club Leader".

"The full time Leader of a Boys' Club (or, as he is sometimes called Warden or Manager) over the age of 25 occupies a position and not always understood by people unfamiliar with Club work. "What does he do in the daytime?" it is asked, "Since his Club is only open in the evenings?" This memorandum attempts to answer this question, and adds some general observations on the conditions of service that should apply.

Clubs have not been produced to any uniform pattern, either as regards size of premises, membership capacity, type of district, nature or degree of public support, or relationship with any sponsoring bodies, and hence the duties of their Leaders are not always the same.

Club Leadership is a vocation, and it would be as alien to its nature to draw up a list of duties and a schedule of hours for a Leader to follow. No good Leader would think of counting his hours of work. Reasonable precautions must, of course, be taken to see that a Leader does not become slack or inefficient.

Duties and Hours of Work.
Evenings and Weekends. Most Clubs with full time Leaders are open on five or six nights a week, Monday to Friday and generally either Saturday or Sunday between the hours of 6.30 and 10pm. It is desirable that a Leader should normally be present whenever the Club is open; this involves his presence for about 20 hours a week. He will need to be at the Club for not less than fifteen minutes before the Club opens and for the same time after the closing hour, this brings his hours of work in the evenings to 23 hours. In addition his Saturday afternoons will be spent with his football or cricket teams, and these duties including travelling, will absorb an average of four hours a week. The Club will also run weekend camps for its members on most weekends in the summer, and will have an annual camp of not less than one week's duration.

Many Clubs are open until 10.30pm for their older members, and run special clubs for schoolboys on one or two nights a week which starts at 5.30pm, it may safely be assumed that the evening and weekend work of a paid Club Leader will absorb an average of thirty hours a week, in personally leading or supervising the activities of the Clubs members.

It is of the essence of Club work that when the Club is open the Club Leader should be free from office and secretarial work to concentrate on his real work "Club Leadership". Much of his time in the Club will be taken up with individual boys, personal interviews of new members and talks with the boys about a host of things, discovering directly or indirectly whether their new job is satisfactory, why they are looking unfit or worried, why they are not saving in the Club bank, why their subscriptions are not up to date, why they have lost interest in this activity or what has happened to their friend who has been missing since last week. It is clearly impossible to catalogue work such as this and yet it is the most important thing a Club Leader can do.

It is through this that he can establish the right relationship of friendship and become an influence in his member's lives. It is only to the Club Leader who has time to talk with each of his members that the individual boy will turn with the many problems and difficulties that most boys have during adolescence and their first years at work.

He will be constantly about the Club, dropping in on all the classes and activities. Perhaps joining in the P. T. Class now and again, showing visitors around the Club, discussing problems with the Club helpers. To accompany his teams to play indoor games against other Clubs and to meet other Club Leaders and share experiences with them. To maintain Club discipline, keeping a watchful eye on the troublesome boy and probably will take the Sunday Club Service and the Evening Prayers, if the Club have them.

Daytime.
The Club Leader is differently occupied but no less busy in the daytime. If the Club has a membership of 150 to 250 boys the Club Leader will spend most of the time in his office. Some of his everyday jobs are: –
Keeping the Club Accounts.

General Administration and Organisation.

Compiling Minutes for the Clubs Management Committee Meeting.

Organising Special events at the Club such as The Annual Club Display, Gymnastics or Boxing Tournaments, Pantomimes, Parents' Night, Christmas Party & Annual Summer Camp outings at Wark and Rothbury.

Visits to outside contacts.

All in a day for a Club Leader.
Certainly the host of activities described by the founder members seem to indicate that Sandy Laws was a fully occupied man between 1938 and 1952 when he left Wallsend Boys' Club.

In the last months of the war, in March 1945, the club was able to sign a lease for the land which they occupied. The lease was agreed between the Mayor of Wallsend, representing the corporation, and the Trustees of the club. These still included Sheriton Clements Swan, and Norman McLeod Hunter, as well as William George Pearson, the Welfare superintendent of the shipyards.

17- THIS LEASE is made the seventeenth day of March one thousand
nine hundred and forty-five BETWEEN THE MAYOR ALDERMEN AND BURGESSES
OF THE BOROUGH OF WALLSEND (hereinafter called "the Corporation")
of the one part and SHERITON CLEMENTS SWAN Shipbuilder NORMAN
McLEOD HUNTER Shipbuilder and WILLIAM GEORGE PEARSON Welfare
Superintendent all of the Shipyard Wallsend aforesaid and HENRY
BRAND of 6 Ashwood Crescent Walkerville in the City and County
of Newcastle upon Tyne Schoolmaster Trustees of the Wallsend
Boys' Club (hereinafter called "the Club") of the other part
WITNESSETH as follows :-

1. IN consideration of the rent hereinafter reserved and the
covenants on the part of the Club hereinafter contained the
Corporation hereby demises unto the Club ALL THAT piece of
land situate on the West side of Station Road Wallsend in the
County of Northumberland containing an area of 2350 square yards
or thereabouts and which said piece of land is delineated on the
plan annexed hereto and thereon coloured round with pink
TOGETHER with the right to erect a wooden building thereon in
accordance with the plans previously approved by the Corporation
TO HOLD the said premises unto the Club for the term of TEN YEARS
from the 1st day of April 1939 the Club YIELDING AND PAYING therefor
during the said term the yearly rent of £1 and thereafter from
year to year (subject to three months notice to quit on either
side) at the said rent or in the event of such premises ceasing
to be used as a Boys' Club then as from such date in the event of
such date being within 10 years the first payment being due on the
said 1st day of April 1939

2. THE Club hereby covenants with the Lessor as follows :-
(a) To pay all rates and taxes of a recurring nature charged upon
or payable in respect of the demised premises during the said
term and to keep the Lessor indemnified from and against the same
(b) To keep the demised premises and all additions thereto in
good and substantial repair and condition throughout the said
term
(c) That the said premises shall only be used for purposes

connected with and in accordance with the Rules for the time being
of the Club
(d) That no part of the land nor any buildings for the time being
thereon shall be used for the sale supply or distribution of
intoxicating liquors or in such manner as to be a nuisance annoyance
or damage to the owners or occupiers of other property in the
neighbourhood
(e) Not to assign or underlet or part with the possession of the
land or premises or any part thereof without the consent in
writing of the Corporation
(f) At the cost of the Club to execute and do all such sanitary
and other works (if any) as the Corporation may from time to time
lawfully require to be executed upon or in respect of the premises
in good order to abate a nuisance or for any other purpose under
any statutory provision in that behalf

3. THE Corporation hereby covenants with the Club that the Club
paying the rent hereby reserved and performing and observing the
covenants and conditions hereinbefore contained shall quietly hold
and enjoy the demised premises during the term hereby created
without any interruption by the Corporation or any person claiming
through under or in trust for the Corporation
IN WITNESS whereof the Trustees have hereunto set their hands and
seals the day and year first before written

SIGNED SEALED AND DELIVERED by)
the said Sheriton Clements Swan } SHERITON C. SWAN   L.S.
in the presence of)

  C.F. TURNBULL,
   4 Berwick Hill Road,
   Ponteland, Newcastle.

SIGNED SEALED AND DELIVERED by)
the said Norman McLeod Hunter } N.M. HUNTER   L.S.
in the presence of)

  W.G. PEARSON

SIGNED SEALED AND DELIVERED by)
the said William George Pearson } WILLIAM G. PEARSON   L.S.
in the presence of)

  A. WAIT,
  "Bemersyde,"
   Sunderland Road, South Shields.
   Insurance Manager

Wallsend Boys' Club lease for land.

Chapter 4 - The Late Forties and Early Fifties: more Pantomimes and the growth of Football

The end of the war in 1945 did not immediately change the social conditions in which most people were living. Although there was the promise of better times ahead, a promise that was at least partly fulfilled with the birth of the Welfare State in 1948, most people in Wallsend continued to live fairly simple lives throughout the 1950s. Certainly in the first half of the decade there was still a mood of 'austerity', with rationing continuing and few luxuries around.

The Wallsend Boys' Club pantomimes continued in the old tradition from 1946 to 1950.

In 1946 the Seventh Annual Pantomime, "Puss in Boots" took place.

This was again a sell out.

In 1946 Sandy would bring friends from the Palace Theatre in the Haymarket at Newcastle to help apply make-up to the cast of the pantomime. He would also take privileged members to the Palace Theatre to work backstage. Jack Carruthers and George Charlton were two of the lucky members to go. Dress rehearsals the day before the WBC pantomime's first night were always chaotic, with Sandy pulling his hair out in frustration. But on opening night everything seemed to run smoothly. Each year Sandy thought of new ways of squeezing money from the audience, selling programmes, ice creams and so on.

In January 1949 Wallsend Boys' Club Presented their 10th Annual Pantomime, "**Dick Whittington & His Cat**". Written, Staged and produced by "Sandy".

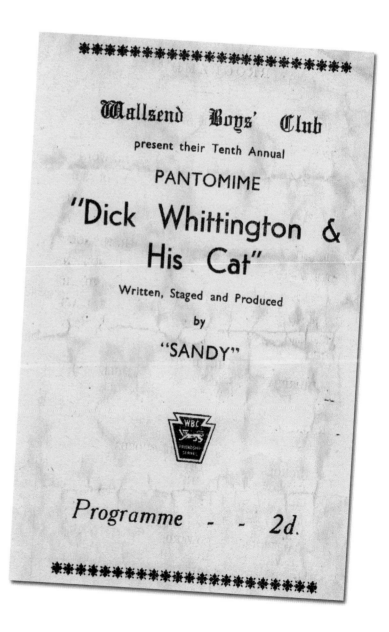

Wallsend Boys' Club present their Tenth Annual PANTOMIME "Dick Whittington & His Cat" Written, Staged and Produced by "SANDY"

Programme - - 2d.

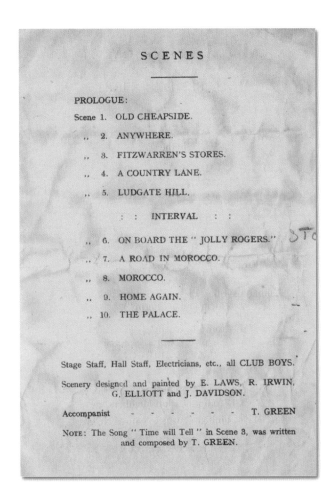

SCENES

PROLOGUE:

Scene 1. OLD CHEAPSIDE.

,, 2. ANYWHERE.

,, 3. FITZWARREN'S STORES.

,, 4. A COUNTRY LANE.

,, 5. LUDGATE HILL.

: : INTERVAL : :

,, 6. ON BOARD THE " JOLLY ROGERS."

,, 7. A ROAD IN MOROCCO.

,, 8. MOROCCO.

,, 9. HOME AGAIN.

,, 10. THE PALACE.

Stage Staff, Hall Staff, Electricians, etc., all CLUB BOYS.

Scenery designed and painted by E. LAWS, R. IRWIN, G. ELLIOTT and J. DAVIDSON.

Accompanist - - - - - - T. GREEN

NOTE: The Song " Time will Tell " in Scene 3, was written and composed by T. GREEN.

PROGRAMME

CAST IN ORDER OF APPEARANCE:

Demon Rat	H BELL
Fairy Crystal	R. WORTH
Alderman Fitzwarren	H. DOBSON
Captain Bloodshed	R. OLIVER
The Mate	K. MURPHY
Idle Jack	R. NICHOLS
Dick Whittington	R. DOBSON
Felix (The Cat)	J. GARDNER
Martha (The Cook)	E. LAWS
The Emperor of Morocco	H. DOBSON

THE PIRATES:

M. MURPHY	R. LANE	P. MULLEN
P. JONES	J. WAKE	D. BALBIRNIE
R. GIBBONS	H. BROWNLEE	V. FINLAY
R. SNELL		N. ARMSTRONG

" LADIES " IN THE CHORUS

F. NICHOLS	H. RILEY	J. POULTER
A. CAMPBELL	J. SWAN	R. McCARTHY
J. LINDSAY		J. McFARLANE

GENTLEMEN:

G. CATTERICK	S. EDWARDS	L. SLOAN
A. BLAYNEY	C. RICHARDSON	L. COLLINS
E. DYER		K. TRAIN

Programme for Dick Whittington and His Cat 1949.

The cast of Dick Whittington and his Cat 1949.

Jimmy Swan in Pantomime 1949.

Wallsend Boys' Club Scarborough trip 1949.
Back Row: Jonna Mitchell, Ray Marr, TBC.
Middle Row: Ray Watson, Jackie Taylor,
Tom Wedderburn, Fred Tate, Alan Humphries.
Front Row: TBC, Jack Scott, Sandy Laws, TBC

1949/1950 Football Team

Old Boys – here is a photograph of the now famous Wallsend Boys' Club football team as it was in the season 1949-50. As you will see, they were winning cups even then. The club then was just a wooden hut on the same site as it is now.

Advertising at that pantomime was Wallsend Boys' Club's first "Pantomime Ball" to be held on 17th January. This was hailed as a 'first' for Wallsend. Tickets cost 4/-, with music by the "Premier Dance Band", and dancing from 8pm until 1am. There were spot prizes and 'lucky' tickets, with a 'perm' being among the prizes on offer. Clearly therefore the club was not restricting entry to boys only! Prizes were presented by Newcastle United's great hero Jackie Milburn, in the middle of his first season as an England player. As a reminder of how times have changed, it is worth noting that at the height of his fame Jackie earned only £17 a week at Newcastle United.

After being demobbed in 1949 Ray 'Pang' Oliver recalls practically living at the club. He was now a volunteer helper rather than a member and remembers that when Sandy Laws, still the club leader, was not on the premises it was left in the hands of himself and other volunteer helpers.

Ray's particular area of expertise was gymnastics instruction, not surprising considering his own skill in that area. He took the Physical Education training sessions two nights a week, Tuesday and Thursday. The gym in the club had a vaulting horse, springboard, parallel bars and a pommel horse. The floor was covered with three coconut mats with a softer mat rolled over the top of them.

As Ray points out, if you landed on an exposed coconut mat you would be ripped apart. The numbers in the P.E. class ranged from 16 to 20 and they would turn up religiously for their training sessions. The Physical Training Team headed by instructor Ray were often asked to perform gymnastic displays at the N. A. B. C. sports day at the Ringtons playing fields. They also performed at West Street Residents Association and at the North East Electric Supply Company situated in Kings Road. Members of the team included Norman Thain, Syd Oliver, Lew Grey and Ian McFarland. The P. E. Team also entered club competitions within the N. A. B. C. every year but unfortunately Wallsend

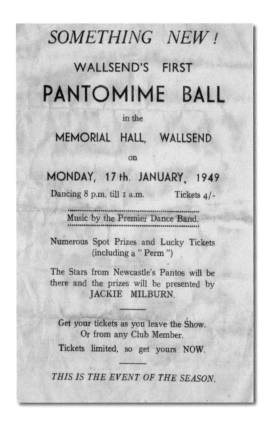

Ray (Pang) Oliver 1945.

Boys' Club were never lucky enough to win but managed to finish runners up twice. The clubs gymnasium would regularly be hired out on Saturdays to Swan Hunters badminton teams from 2pm to 10pm with Swan's lads providing their own flood lighting.

Other activities in the club at the time included table tennis, with the club having two tables. There was a rule that at 9pm members would vacate the tables to allow those members who had been at night classes to have a game before the club closed at 10pm. Ray Oliver also acted as football coach until he left the club in 1952. He would take the players out on jogging sessions, running down Station Road to North Road, along North Road to West Street, up West Street as far as Whitley Road (the 'old Coast Road') and then right to the top of Station Road before heading south again to the club building. One night Ray had sprained his ankle so couldn't accompany the boys, sending them out with team captain Mel Murphy instead. Hobbling out to check on their progress he found them taking a huge short cut from West Street along Dorset Avenue.

They were promptly sent back on the proper route with Mel getting a roasting from Ray for allowing this 'mutiny'.

Wallsend Boys' Club Pantomime Mother Goose 1950.
Ernest (Sandy) Laws, Len Gray, Andy Campbell, Sos Hunter, Jim Marshall, Len Massie, Peter Terrace, Norman Armstrong, Seppy Armstrong, Syd Edwards, Joe Dyche and Foster Nichols as Mother Goose.

Norman Livingstone story

Football was of course becoming even more popular in the North East by the 1950s. Perhaps this was partly because of the success of Newcastle United, or perhaps it was because of slightly more leisure time. Wallsend Boys' Club had junior teams organised at that time into two age groups, 14-16 and 16-18. Norman Livingstone has clear memories of his time in the older squad in the 1951-1952 season. He recalls that in 1950 Dave Henderson (Right Half), Robert Rowe (Goalkeeper) and he (Left Back) were apprentices at the North Eastern Marine and playing for Wallsend St. Peters 14 to 16 age group. Being a church club they brought in a rule that you had to go to church on a Sunday in order to play for the team the following Saturday. Also working at the N.E.M. was Fred Mason who was a toolmaker. He was also the manager of the under 18 team at Wallsend Boys' Club. He wanted to improve his squad so he asked if they wanted to join the Boys' Club. Hence the team for the 1951/52 season.

Norman says they were never very active members as they were mainly there for the football but he did manage to make a bookcase in John Haldon's woodwork class.

They developed into a good team and were soon in the top three of the league along with St. Columba's and North Shields East End. The team varied but Norman remembers it as Robert Rowe or Danny O'Fee in goal, Alan Southwell right back, Norman Livingstone left back, Dave Henderson right half, Peter Watson centre half, D. Duggan left half, Jimmy Swan outside right (sometimes), Ronnie Adams inside right, Andy Campbell (Captain) centre forward, John Jenson inside left, John Moffitt or Bob Henderson outside left.

John Jenson, John Moffitt and Bob Henderson were also apprentices at N.E.M. Jimmy Swan was the "Super Sub". He could play anywhere and was a terrier according to Norman. They beat North Shields East End 2-1 away at the end of the season and Norman scored with a penalty and Jimmy Swan scored the winner.

Peter Watson and Andy Campbell were selected to play for the N.A.B.C. representative team.

Wallsend Boys' Club played their home games on the Western School field. They would change in the Boys' Club on Station Road and walk round to the pitch through the allotments, carrying the corner flags etc. Their strip colours were red tops with white sleeves and a white collar, which was provided by the Club, but they had to buy their own blue shorts (ex-Army) and red and white hooped socks, as well as having to find their own way to the away matches.

Norman says he always had admiration for the goalkeeper as the goalmouths never had any grass on them and it was either a mud bath or rock hard to dive about on. During the season a trip was arranged to play York Boys' Club in York. The team had to pay for the trip themselves but one of the team (Bandy Bob Henderson) could not afford to pay for the trip. His mother was a widow and he was the only wage earner in the house on apprentice wages. To save money Bandy Bob would walk from his North Shields home to work in Wallsend and walk back to North Shields at the end of his shift.

The club arranged a fund raising dance at the Boys' Club to raise some money towards the York trip. They held a free raffle on the night, with the prize being a free trip to York for the football match. A volunteer picked the lucky persons name out of the hat and amazingly Bandy Bobs name was on the winning ticket. When checking the names in the hat after the dance was over, we found that Bandy Bobs name was on every ticket. Norman thinks they had a very sympathetic dance organiser. They went to York by bus on the Saturday morning, played the game in the afternoon beating them comprehensively and had a night out in York at the funfair. At 16/17 years of age they did not go in to pubs. They slept overnight at their clubhouse and their team sponsor "Terry's Chocolates" treated them to a delicious Sunday lunch.WBC invited them to a return fixture and beat them again. On the Saturday night it was pantomime season at the Boys' Club so the team invited them to watch one of the shows. They slept at the Boys' Club on the Saturday night and on the Sunday morning were taken to the newly opened Tyne Pedestrian Tunnel. The Club could not afford to give their visitors Sunday lunch so each member of the team took a member of the visiting team to his home for lunch with his family.

Towards the end of the season the games were building up so they played one team away on Easter Saturday beating them 11-0 and arranged for the reverse home fixture against the same team on the Easter Monday. When they turned up for the Easter Monday game the names on the team sheet were the same as the Saturday but the players were entirely different, being a lot bigger and older.

On talking to a couple of their players Norman says they found out that the team they had sent was their Sunday morning league team. The score was 2-2 at half time but WBC scored 6 in the second half to beat them 8-2.

WBC team won the league title with the help of a little "Arrangement". The last game had to be played before the official end of the season and the opponents could not field a full side. As WBC would have beaten them comfortably, team manager Fred Mason "arranged" a win with the opponent's team manager and hence the two league points were gained to win the 1951/52 league title.

Unfortunately success meant that local scouts poached players away from the Wallsend Boys' Club team. Andy Campbell was poached by the Rising Sun Colliery team, which was one of the leading amateur teams in the area at that time, and he was just one of many players poached away from the team. Norman comments that manager Fred Mason and Coach Ray "Pang" Oliver must have been very disappointed that their successful team broke up so quickly.

Wallsend Boys' Club 1951/52

Standing: Fred Mason (team manager) Peter Watson, Dave Henderson, Alan Southwell, Danny O-fee, Jimmy Huggan, Steve Turner, Robert Rowe, M Wright, Ronnie Adams, Ray Oliver (coach)
Sitting: John Jenson, Bob Dudding, Andy Campbell, (captain) Norman Livingstone, Jim Swan, Ken Elliot.

An inventory of items in the club premises taken in May 1952 gives some idea of the range of activities still undertaken.

Inventory of items in Wallsend Boys' Club. At the 31st May 1952.

Main Hall:
8 long forms, 1 piano, 1 swivel chair, 1 netball goal (Fixed)

Stage:
1 front curtain and backcloth, 1 set of pillars, 3 steps, 2 rostrums

Library:
1 settee, 2 basket chairs, 1 leather easy chair, 3 wooden chairs, 2 tables, 9 pictures, assorted books & 1 pair of curtains

Showers:
P.T. Equipment. 1 vaulting horse, 1 vaulting box, 1 boxing ring, 1 punch ball & stand, 1 badminton net, 1 netball goal & 3 mats

Games Room:
1 billiard table, 1 rest, 6 cues, balls (stolen), 1 iron, 2 table tennis tables, 6 bats, 4 balls, 3 tables, 12 chairs, 1 wooden settee, 17 folding chairs, 9 pairs curtains & 1 dart board

Canteen:
1 clock, 1 vantas machine, 2 silver cups, 22 glasses (1 at police station), 14 small cups, 9 large cups, 12 saucers, 3 plates, 1 tea urn, 1 large tea pot, 1 oven, assorted cutlery, 2 enamel dishes, 1 set of domino's, 1 set of draughts, darts (stolen)

Office:
12 football strips, 1 football, 1 bookcase, assorted books (Plays etc), 3 chairs, 1 cupboard, 3 pictures, note paper etc, files, 1 rubber stamp & 2 pads, 1 paper clipper, 1 pair curtains, 1 first aid box & 1 visitors book

Store cupboard:
1 table, 1 box tags (Flag Day), 1 head guard (Boxing), 10 pairs of boxing gloves, 2 badminton rackets, 2 sets of clubs, 2 medicine balls, 2 camp pans, odd football strips, odd footballs (No Bladders) odd cricket gloves & 1 whitewash brush

Woodwork Room:
5 steel planes, 5 iron saws, 2 dovetail saws, 1 coping saw, 1 keyhole saw, 2 wood spoke shavers, 1 metal spoke shaver (broken), 1 Wood Jack plane, 4 wood smoothing planes, 4 mallets, 2 hammers, 4 gauges, 3 fit squares, 2 screwdrivers, 2 oilstones (1 broken), 5 hand saws, 1 pair of pliers, 13 chisels, 1 brace, ¼ & ½ drill bits, 1 nail pouch & 1 lathe (property of Mr Mason).

Another little reminder of how the immediate post-war years were a very simple age comes with the number of 21st birthday parties and even wedding receptions held in the club premises. Jack Scott's mother sent out formal printed invitations to his 'Coming of Age' party on April 12th 1947, starting at 4pm. Ray Oliver also held his 21st there, and his brother Stan held his wedding reception in the club.

Members older than 18 were known at that time as 'Old Boys'.

In April 26th 1950 the club hosted a celebration of their own 11th birthday.

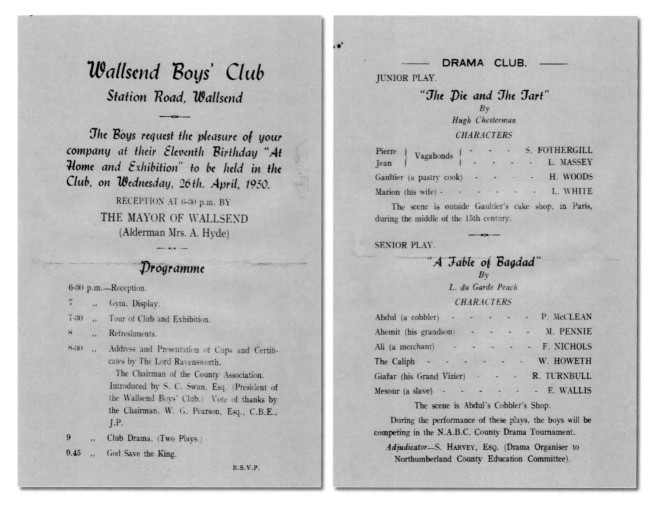

Among the entertainments staged for the Mayor of Wallsend were a gymnastics display, a presentation of various certificates and cups, and two short plays, which were also doubling up as Wallsend Boys' Club's entry into the NABC county drama tournament.

The cups and certificates were presented by Lord Ravensworth, Chairman of the County Association, and the ever present Sheriton C. Swan introduced proceedings as President of the Club.

It is clear that the club intended to continue with its theatrical ventures since in 1957 it was granted a licence from the Borough of Wallsend for the public performance of Music, Singing and Dancing. It is noticeable that this licence was granted to the new club leader, Alan Ruse, Sandy Laws having left in 1952 after being with the club since it opened in 1938.

Ray Oliver also left soon afterwards and took up voluntary work with a youth club in North Shields.

On 26th July 1952 Eddie Young held his Wedding reception at Wallsend Boys' Club.

Eddie (Bunty) Young and his bride Vera outside Wallsend Boys' Club 1952.

Alan Ruse was appointed from 1st June 1952 with a salary of £400 per annum. His contract was for three months in the first instance and would be subject to confirmation at the end of that period when he became eligible for inclusion in the N.A.B.C. insurance and superannuation scheme. His letter of appointment outlined his duties and responsibilities as club leader. It pointed out that the Club was open five nights a week and he was expected to be present at each session with certain reservations. It was emphasised that the Committee attached great importance to the careful keeping of records and to frequent visiting of the Club Members homes and the setting and maintaining the highest possible standards in every aspect of the Clubs life and work.

He had at his disposal the services of a part time manager, the supervision of whose work was also Alan's responsibility.

Alan (skipper) Ruse.
Manager of Wallsend Boys' Club
1952-1957.

The Committee wrote that they very much hoped that he would attract to the Club, a number of suitable voluntary helpers and that he would make the widest possible contacts with people representative of every part of the life in the community. They went on to say that they realised that the Club Leader's work involved a strong sense of vocation and that, like all people who take up work of this kind, the Club Leader is only too prone to sacrifice everything to his work. For that reason they wanted to make it very clear that he took four weeks holiday each year. The period when the Club was in camp would not count as part of his holiday and if he, with the Committee's agreement, assisted at camps organised by the County Association, this period would again not be part of his holiday. In addition the fullest possible opportunities were to be afforded him for attendance at training courses and conferences organised either locally or nationally.

The Committee considered that no club leader could do his job satisfactorily unless he had adequate leisure to recreate himself and to keep abreast of the times and therefore made it a condition of his appointment that he should have free a clear period of 24 hours each week. The committee stated, "You will appreciate that no men working continuously with young people can be fully effective unless he develops his own social life and his own personal interests and that by reserving to yourself the leisure on which the Committee insists you will ultimately be benefiting the Club and your own work. We want to emphasise to you our desire to give you every possible support in your work and to express our hopes for your own happiness and success in the leadership of our club."

THEY LEARN TO MEET THE DUKE

Members of Wallsend Boys Club who are to be presented to the Duke of Gloucester — the Queen's uncle — on his tour of Tyneside in February, are at present receiving 'lessons' on how to behave in front of the Duke.
Said Mr Allan M. Ruse, the Club warden, who is instructing the boys: " Lots of youngsters won't know the correct way to address the Duke.
" We are trying to help them out of this difficulty."

During Alan Ruse's time as club leader the club was visited by the Duke of Gloucester who was patron of the National Association of Boys' Clubs. The Duke was embarking on a whirlwind tour of clubs in Northumberland in February 1956 and included Wallsend in his itinerary.

In spite of the short time spent in the club, the boys were trained how to bow to a royal visitor and seem to have given him a very warm welcome. Leslie White, the 18 year old chairman of the Boys' committee, presented the Duke with a scroll marking his honorary membership of the club and led the other boys in 'three cheers'.

In another little insight into the time, it is interesting to see that the scheduled length of time for the Duke's train journey from London to Newcastle was five and a half hours.

I enclose the programme for the visit of H.R.H. The Duke of Gloucester on the 23rd February. As you will see he is due to arrive at your Boys' Club at 6.55pm. The procedure will be that the Duke of Northumberland, who will be travelling in the police car in front of His Royal Highness, will present you (Mr D. Leete) at the entrance to your Club and you will then present H.R.H. to the following executives of your Club.

        Police Superintendent, G. Bell.
        Mr V. Stevens.
        Mr R. Duncan.
        Mr V. J. McFarlane.
        Mr N. Thain.
        Mr J. Jackson.
        Mr J. Rosborough.
        Mr A. Ruse. (Club Leader).

As you will see, your Club Leader should be the last person to be presented, as he then escorts H.R.H. round the Club. Would you please impress on your Club Leader that we must adhere to the schedule and therefore, he must do his utmost to see that H.R.H. leaves your Club at the time stated on the programme. I am sure you will appreciate that it is essential on a visit of this sort to maintain the times stated.

It is a great honour to this Association for the President of the N.A.B.C, to visit us during our twenty first year, and I am sure you will do all you can to co operate with me to ensure that the visit is a very successful one.

With kind regards,

                              The Hon. Denis G. Berry. Chairman.

"Come on lads, let's have three cheers for our new member" sang out 18 year old Leslie White, chairman of the Boys' committee. Boys in the boxing ring and boys wearing football gear gave three hearty cheers for the new member H.R.H. The Duke of Gloucester, who had just accepted honorary life membership of the club.

Smiling broadly and obviously pleased with the boys' gesture H.R.H. said "Thank you all very much for making me an honorary member of your club. I am very glad to be able to come and visit you and I wish you all the best of luck".

H.R.H. received from Leslie White a scroll inscribed in gilt containing the resolution offering him honorary membership, which was passed at a special meeting of the club committee. H.R.H. was told by Alan Ruse who had escorted him on a tour of the Club that the idea had come from the boys themselves.
In a room where a portrait of his father held an honoured place on the wall, the Duke signed an illuminated vellum document commemorating his visit, which had been painted by an apprentice shipyard draughtsman, Norman Thain, of Hollins Crescent, Wallsend.

Duke of Gloucester on visit to Wallsend Boys' Club 23rd February 1956.
With Club Manager Alan Ruse (centre), and club member George Forbes (right).

Chapter 5 – The later 1950s: Football, boxing and a changing era

By 1958 Wallsend Boys' Club had a new leader in Frank Herdman, who had been appointed on a part-time basis. It was recognised by this time that as times were changing, so would the club have to, at least in some respects.

The club was in fact facing more competition than ever before. The mid-1950s saw the development in Wallsend of youth clubs under the auspices of the National Association of Youth Clubs. Furthermore churches of all denominations were making better provision for younger members and groups like boy scouts and boys' brigade were attracting membership. John McNally suggests in his essay that under the leadership of Frank Herdman it was decided that all apprentices at Swan Hunters shipyard would be made members and pay weekly subscriptions to help the bank balance. (Whether the apprentices objected to this was not recorded.) Frank Herdman then also introduced some new activities such as motor cycle maintenance, photography and weight lifting. Perhaps more radically, girls were admitted one night a week and on a Saturday evening for a dance. These Saturday night dances attracted about 300 young people according to John McNally and canteen sales were very high. (No alcohol of course.)

Frank Herdman Wallsend Boys' Club Manager 1958/59.

By the late 1950s skiffle was in vogue, and the Boys' club had its own band, the Red Planets. In 1958 they were chosen to take part in the annual Frankie Vaughan Boys' Club variety club at the Royal Festival Hall in London. 20 year old John White, another member and a miner, were also invited to take part. John was a comedian and was given a ten minute solo spot whilst the Red Planets accompanied Frankie in a song. The local press pointed out that this was the first time anyone from north of Birmingham had been chosen for the variety show. (You might wonder if this was something to do with the length of the journey!)

As the craze for skiffle grew several local bands gained permission to use the club premises for practice sessions. One of these groups, The Animals, went on to realise the dream of many young men by making their name locally and then travelling to the 'Big City', London, before becoming famous world wide with their hit "The House of the Rising Sun" – which had no connection with the only remaining Wallsend pit!

In October 1958, the club put on "Stairway to the Stars" at the Memorial Hall. This was a way of raising money for the club, which by that time was becoming a major preoccupation.

As early as 1951 the club had had to raise £150 each year towards running costs of £600. This doesn't sound a lot by today's standards, but of course the average wage at the time was only £3/8 shillings a week.

The club was supported by grants from the Education Committee and also by donations from Swan Hunter and Wigham Richardson and from Wallsend Slipway (£50 each per annum at that time.)

Sheriton Swan also provided a personal covenant of £5 per year as well as proceeds from the sale of his fruit and vegetables.

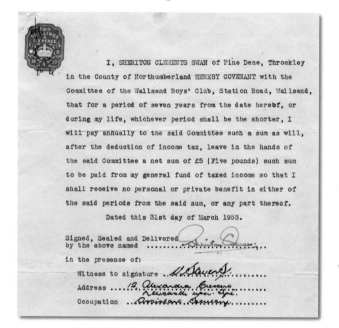

Sheriton Clements Swan's Covenant to Wallsend Boys' Club in 1953.

Paying the sum of £5.00 a year after tax for life.

In 1956 the club had only £40 in the bank. Nevertheless, by 1958 in his report to the club committee, Frank Herdman was able to say that the club was going from strength to strength. It had £580 in a deposit account plus a small amount in a current account. The treasurer, Mr F. Dixon, was able to claim that "the financial position of the club has never looked rosier," and that he had every confidence that this would continue as long as they could keep Frank Herdman as club leader.

Football also continued to play an important part in club life with the season of 1956-1957 particularly significant.

Northumberland Junior Football Association, East Division, Honours Certificate. Season 1956/57.

This is to certify that **Jim Richardson** of Wallsend Boys' Club was selected at centre half to play for the Division in the following representative game.

East Northumberland versus Sunderland Y.O.C. at Sunderland (Roker Park) on December 26th 1956.

April 1957. The giants of junior soccer will do battle.

Wallsend Boys' Club v North Shields.

Write up by Wallsend Boys' Club's manager Frank Herdman on the team to play North Shields in the "game of the season".

Wallsend Boys' Club Football Team: -

T. Gibson, the goalkeeper who is right on form at the moment. He is also keen on boxing and is the Northumberland junior champion.

B. Rowe, right back and a good strong player. He is a former Wallsend Schoolboy player.

M. Cuskern left back who also plays for Newcastle Boys and Northumberland Boys.

T. Rowland's, right half and skipper. Resolute and methodical is just the type to lead the team.

J. Richardson, centre half, one of the stars of the team. He is captain of Newcastle Boys and Northumberland Boys. Has played for East Northumberland Youth F.A. and is an England trialist.

K. Connelly, left half is the football artist of the team and is another former Wallsend Schoolboy player.

J. McRae, outside right who can be a match winner. He is always looking for that scoring chance.

J. Blacklock, inside right of Wallsend Grammar School is a tall intelligent player.

J. Kirtley, centre forward has scored more than 40 goals this season.

H. Wilkinson, inside left is a 90-minute player.

G. Forbes, outside left a two-footed player and is hard to move off the ball.

Pictured before their game last week are members of the Wallsend Boys' Club. Front row, left to right; McRae, Blacklock, Rowland, Kirtley, Forbes. Back row, left to right; Wilkinson, Richardson, Murrey, Cuskern, Gibson, Rowe, Connolly.

Wallsend Evening News April 1957.

Apart from football, boxing also continued to be a strong point for Wallsend Boys' Club. Tony Corkhill was a key member of the club at this time and his own words give us a marvellously vivid, and funny, account of life as a member of the boxing team in the late 1950s.

Tony Corkhill's story

"A crisp February night in 1957 and I crunched my way up the path of Wallsend Boys' Club for my nightly training session. I was a fifteen year old amateur boxer with a regime straight out of the Ghurkhas' survival manual. Ten minutes skipping, twenty minutes shadow boxing, thirty press-ups, running on the spot and a few runs round the hall would get me warmed up before putting on the gloves and sparring round after round with each of the other lads who were equally as keen as I was.

Just as I was about to go into the changing room, Frank 'Skipper' Herdman called me into his office.

"If it's about my subs I'll pay it all next week", I said, thinking that that was the issue he wanted to discuss. The subs at that time were sixpence a week and my arrears were somewhere on the half a crown mark.

"No Tony, it's not that, I know you'll pay", said Frank, clearing a chair for me to sit on. "How would you like to represent the Boys' Club in the regional finals? It's in three weeks time in Burnley."

Represent the Boys' Club? Regional finals? Burnley? Yes to all three. I would have said yes had they been held in Outer Mongolia, never mind Burnley.

Frank looked pleased and said he'd let me know all the arrangements when he heard from the Boys' Club Association. I trained extra hard that night. Heavens, this was like being picked for Newcastle to play at Wembley.

A few nights later I was throwing the medicine ball around when, out of the corner of my eye, I saw two figures entering the club. I recognised them immediately, - Jackie Wright and Tommy 'Tucker' Moulden. Both had boxed professionally during the depression and were still well respected in local boxing circles. They had come along to the club to pass on their extensive and valuable skills and we would be only too keen to listen.

Jackie had not, apparently, altered much since his heyday thirty odd years ago and still, it was said, packed a punch like a steam hammer.

He had managed to hold on to a full head of sleek black hair which made him look ten years younger. Tucker, although appearing unsteady on his feet at times was a dapper little man of about five feet two and often wore a homberg hat as he strutted off most nights to the Penny Wet bar in Wallsend, smiling and nodding to everyone as he went. Both were men of a friendly disposition and never appeared bitter that they had fought in an era when a ten shilling purse was the norm. Had they been around today they would have had the opportunity to be rich men. I was pleased when they said that they would be coming along to Burnley.

The big day arrived and we shivered outside the club as we waited for the coach from Hollings Garage on North Road. Jackie's chilblains were playing up and Tucker had a dewdrop on the end of his nose that was beginning to freeze. It had snowed all night and frozen solid around dawn. The blizzard conditions were set to continue well into the day. We must have looked a sorry sight, standing like a bunch of snowmen and facing what was to be a six hour coach trip. It was a toss-up who would reach us first, the coach or a St Bernard.

About twenty minutes late, the coach crawled nervously down the Comrades' Club bank, the driver desperate not to slither into the burn on the left side of the road. We gave a half hearted cheer as we piled on, the younger lads like myself filling up the back seat and the old timers up front talking to the driver. We had to pick up more people on the way, six at Walker and a dozen or so at Gateshead.

After a few miles we began to thaw out and even warm up. Up the front, the boxing stories were flying about, thick and fast. Whilst at the back the talk was all about the latest hits by Tommy Steele, Bill Haley and the Everley Brothers. As well as the new range of Winkle Pickers that Timpsons had in for thirty nine and eleven.

I drew deeply on my fourth Woodbine. Tucker eyeballed me from the front seat and came rushing up the aisle. "Put that out", he said, waving a finger. "Woodbines will do you no good at all. When we stop for a cup of tea at Darlington get yourself a packet of Capstan full strength. They'll make you cough and you'll get rid of loads of phlegm". This may be hard to believe these days, but in the pre-politically correct fifties just about everyone smoked, unaware of the health risks that are now part of every day education.

Everyone on our coach certainly smoked and by Darlington the air was blue and, due to the high nicotine content, we must have looked like a group of tourists who had just come back from a week in Benidorm as we got off for our break.

Hours later we arrived in Burnley and we cleared the condensation from the window to see what it looked like. It was grey. The buildings were grey, the people were grey. It looked like a 1947 Ealing film. There were tall chimneys and factories all around. They were grey too. It was like watching 'Brief Encounter' only with more smoke and steam. I expected to see Margaret Rutherford walking by, or was it Celia Johnston?

We found the venue, Burnley Town Hall, after a while and went inside for refreshments. It was now only a couple of hours before the show started and butterflies and 'What am I doing here?' were beginning to invade the nervous system. Jackie and Tucker went away to get the programme. They looked happy when they came back. I was second on the bill and was matched against a local lad named Horace Jowsey. Tucker reckoned that I had a great chance. His logic was that a boxer named Horace was like being a bricklayer named Mavis. Boxers weren't called Horace. They were called Rocky, or Kid, or Jersey Joe. I thanked Tucker for his confidence but decided to reserve judgement until I met the lad.

We watched from behind a curtain as the crowd filled the auditorium. Row upon row of cauliflower ears and broken noses took up most of the ringside seats whilst civic dignitaries and their lady wives perched on the balcony. Jackie and Tucker pulled me to one side to talk tactics. If I got knocked down they told me to look across to my corner immediately. As the referee counted, Tucker would point to the floor until he was satisfied that I'd had a few seconds to recover my composure, then he'd point upwards and I'd jump up and resume the fight. It seems that a lot of fights are lost because the boxer gets up just a second or two too early. Sound advice, but I hoped I wouldn't need it.

Whatever my fate, I would find out soon because the programme had been rearranged and I was on first. I climbed between the ropes into the ring and caught my first glimpse of Horace. He certainly didn't look soft as Tucker had forecast. He was six inches taller than me and looked about ten years older. The crowd all seemed to know him as he waved confidently to them from his corner.

Cheers filled the hall as the referee announced, "In the red corner, Horace Jowsey". By contrast, you could hear a pin drop when he announced, "In the blue corner, Tony Corkhill".

As I stood in the corner waiting for the bell, Tucker's words of wisdom came into my head. Round one, get to know your opponent. Round two, score points. Round three, finish him off. Unfortunately, nobody had told Horace, who, in a few seconds time, would be doing it all in reverse.

The bell clanged and we moved forward and sportingly touched gloves to commence the bout. The sound of the bell was to be the last thing I heard comprehensibly for the rest of the night. We exchanged a few tentative punches as we settled in to a rhythm. I flicked out a left which caught Horace bang on the end of his nose which did not please him. Temporarily blinded by this action he set into motion his defence mechanism. Page one; punch your opponent into submission.

Horace came at me with the power of a threshing machine. Right followed left followed right. Horace was annoyed and I was being swamped. Thump, bang, thump, bang, and again. I was on the canvas with a halo of stars round my head. I looked over to the corner. Tucker was pointing to the floor as arranged. Three, four, five, stay down, five, six, seven stay down, eight, up you get.

Dizzily I got to my feet only to be met by another barrage from Horace. My visit to the floor had not appeased him and he was now baying like a bloodhound. Besides, he did not like fights that lasted longer than thirty seconds. Down I went again, not knowing which part of my body to hold. It hurt everywhere. Jackie and Tucker indicated once again that I stay down till the ref counted to eight. Instinct and stupidity were beginning to take hold as I got to my feet again. It seemed the more I got up, the madder Horace became and he came at me again, thump, knock, bang. I was beginning to lose all reasoning and sensibility. I didn't know where I was or who I was.

There was something grossly unfair about all this. Why should Horace have seventeen fists when I've only got two? Why are his gloves lined with tungsten carbide? Why does he keep hitting me when we've only just met?

I'm back on the floor again with Jackie and Tucker furiously beckoning me to stay down permanently. But I don't know because I'm dreamily looking to the wrong corner. I get back on my feet and the ref looks at me closely.

He asks if I'm OK. I nod yes, but would have done so if he'd asked me if I was Bulgarian. We box on, and Horace starts to realise that he's better than even money to win this one. A ring of multi-coloured flashes accompany me to the floor and stay with me till I'm counted out.

**It's down and out for Tony Corkhill at Burnley Town Hall with Jackie Wright
on the left and Tucker Moulden on the right.**

I came to under a cold shower, having been sat there by Tucker who swore by this sudden re-awakening although it would be hard to find any recommendation in the medical journal. Horace came in and asked me if I was all right. I told him that I would have been if he hadn't knocked me out.

We had a laugh and a handshake and there were no hard feelings. We went back in to watch the rest of the bouts although I dozed off to sleep with concussion.

Our party and others stayed overnight at Burnley police station, sleeping on mattresses on the floor. After an early breakfast we boarded the coach for the long journey back to Wallsend.

The weather had worsened overnight and the grim, grey chimneys stood out eerily against the background of smoke, steam and snow. Although L. S. Lowry was yet to become a household name, his entire catalogue of landscapes were being unrolled before our eyes as we slowly travelled out of Burnley. I ached all over. I had two black eyes and didn't dare have a Capstan full strength as the coughing hurt my ribs.

After a refreshment stop around mid-morning, I noticed that Jackie and Tucker and a few more old timers up the front were opening the large wicker hamper which had been in the boot on the way down. I had been told that it contained "various boxing requisites" but noticed that it smelled more of hops than liniment and embrocation.

An older and wiser Tony Corkhill.

Besides, I remembered that I had at the time wondered why it had been picked up round the back of 'Blenkies' off-licence beside the Buddle School. All was revealed soon enough when the bottle opener was found. Bottles of Mackeson and Oatmeal stout came from the bottom of the hamper like off a production line. Us young uns didn't mind.

The old boys had been good enough to come all the way to Burnley with us so let them have their fun. When I went to Burnley to box for the Boys' Club I was at the start of my working life. I am now a year away from retirement. It is hard to believe that a lifetime has passed since that day Horace Jowsey beat me to a pulp.

A couple of years later I found out that Horace, after beating me went on to become all-England champion and later turned professional, which made me feel a lot better knowing I had been beaten by a classy opponent.

Tucker died many years ago and Jackie sadly passed away only recently having lived to a ripe old age."

Serious Fire Hits Club

Sadly, all of this activity suffered a setback on June 9th 1959 when the club building was gutted by a serious blaze. The hall and gym suffered extensive damage, and much sports equipment was lost. Ironically the club had just spent £600 on renovation and redecoration, the first since it's opening in 1939. Among the items saved however were all the trophies won over the years, and the framed certificate marking the honorary membership of the Duke of Gloucester. These had been stored in a fire-proof safe.

The mood of the club seems to have been determined as well as dismayed.

After seeing flames almost completely gut the club Frank Herdman was quoted in the local press as surveying the charred ruins and saying, "We will just have to start all over again. The Club will go on."

The press account continued; "Beginning at 5pm the fire swept through the hall of the timber building in Station Road, then spread slowly into the main building.

Although Wallsend Fire Brigade had the blaze under control within half an hour, extensive damage was done to the hall and gym and to sports equipment stored there."

A social evening for 100 members and friends of the Club, planned for that night, had to be cancelled. Many turned up and saw firemen in the ruined building. Later they helped to clear away the mess.

A meeting of the management committee was scheduled for the Monday evening when Mr Herdman was to have reported upon successful completion of the renovation and decorating work at the Club.

Mr Frank Davidson, licensee of the nearby Dorset Arms, who saw smoke rising from the back of the building where the boiler house was situated, raised the alarm.

Two tons of coke was stored there but the boiler had not been used for months. At the height of the fire smoke was being blown on to Station Road, which held up the traffic. No one was in the Club at the time, and there were no casualties.

INSPECTING THE DAMAGE

FRIDAY, JUNE 12, 1959

BLAZE GUTS BOYS' CLUB –AFTER A £600 REFIT

WALLSEND Boys' Club will rise again. After seeing flames almost completely gut it on Wednesday, the club leader, Mr. Frank Herdman, surveying the charred ruins, said: "We will just have to start all over again. The club will go on".

Beginning at 5 p.m., the fire swept through the hall of the timber building, in Station Road, then spread slowly into the main building. Although Wallsend Fire Brigade had the blaze under control within half an hour, extensive damage was done to the hall and gym and to sports equipment stored there.

"The whole club had just been renovated and redecorated at a cost of £600—the first time in its 20 years of existence," said Mr. Herdman 'However, we will get over it."

GAVE ALARM

A social evening for 100 members and friends of the club, planned for last night, had to be cancelled. Many turned up and saw firemen in the ruined building. Later they helped to clear away the mess.

A meeting of the management committee was scheduled for Monday evening, when Mr. Herdman was to have reported upon successful completion of the renovation and decorating work at the club.

The alarm was raised by Mr. Frank Davidson, licensee of the nearby Dorset Arms, who saw smoke rising from the back of the building, where the boiler house is situated. Two tons of coke were stored there, but the boiler has not been used this year.

ROYAL MEMBER

At the height of the fire, smoke blown on to Station Road held up traffic. No one was in the club at the time, and there were no casualties.

All the trophies which the club has won were saved as they were stored in a fire-proof safe.

Another important article which survived the blaze was a framed certificate marking

the appointment of the Duke of Gloucester as an honorary life member of the club, on February 23, 1956.

To raise the money needed for the recent work on the premises, the club has held many activities. With a membership of about 150, it has a fine record of achievement.

Among the trophies held by the club are the Northumberland County Senior and Junior Boxing Championship trophies, the YOC League Challenge Cup and the Milburn Cup, an open athletics championship cup.

Wallsend firemen inspecting the damage done to the stage in the main hall of Wallsend Boys' Club, in Station Road, on Wednesday.

Wallsend News Friday 12th June 1959.

BLAZE GUTS BOYS' CL[

We start afresh– leader

WALLSEND Boys' Club will rise again. After seeing flames almost completely gut it last night, club leader Frank Herdman, surveying the charred ruins, said: "We will just have to start all over again. The club will go on".

Beginning at 5 p.m., the fire swept through the hall of the timber building, in Station Road, then spread slowly into the main building. Although Wallsend Fire Brigade had the blaze under control within half an hour, extensive damage was done to the hall and gym and to sports equipment stored there.

"The whole club had just been renovated and redecorated at a cost of £600—the first time in its 20 years of existence," said Mr. Herdman. "However, we will get over it."

A social evening for 100 members and friends of the club, planned for last night, had to be cancelled. Many turned up and saw firemen in the ruined building. Later they helped to clear away the mess.

GAVE ALARM

A meeting of the management committee was scheduled for Monday evening, when Mr. Herdman was to have reported upon successful completion of the renovation and decorating work at the club.

The alarm was raised by Mr. Frank Davidson, licensee of the nearby Dorset Arms, who saw smoke rising from the back of the building, where the boiler house is situated. Two tons of coke were stored there, but the boiler has not been used this year.

At the height of the fire, smoke blown on to Station Road held up traffic. No one was in the club at the time, and there were no casualties.

All the trophies which the club has won were saved as they were stored in a fire-proof safe.

ROYAL MEMBER

Another important article which survived the blaze was a framed certificate marking the appointment of the Duke of Gloucester as an honorary life member of the club, on February 23, 1956.

To raise the money needed for the recent work on the premises, the club has held many activities. With a membership of about 150, it has a fine record of achievement.

Among the trophies held by the club are the Northumberland County Senior and Junior Boxing Championship trophies, the YOC League Challenge Cup and the Milburn Cup, an open athletics championship cup.

Wallsend firemen inspecting the damage done to the stage in the main hall of Boys' Club, at Station Road last night.

Wallsend News Thursday 11th June 1959.

WALLSEND Boys' Club, gutted by fire on Wednesday of last week, has already begun its battle to start afresh. Only eight days after the blaze which destroyed most of the club's equipment, donations totalling more than £70 have come in—plus goods which bring the total to well over £100. And all without canvassing.

Now the club is to ask the Town Council for the lease of the land where its clubhouse is extended.

Then at least £2,500 will have to be raised in about 12 months, to qualify for a Ministerial grant of approximately £8,000 to build a new brick clubhouse.

To raise the money a great effort will be needed and the Wallsend News has been asked to help in launching a fund by the 506 Field Squadron RE (TA) whose headquarters are in Vine Street, Wallsend.

The Commanding Officer, Major C. C. Reed, speaking of the "yeoman service" which the club has rendered to the town, says the squadron will donate £50 to the rebuilding fund.

MAYOR WILL HELP

The Mayor of Wallsend, Coun. J. C. Grogan, has pledged his "whole-hearted support." Donations should be sent to the club's honorary treasurer, Mr. V. Stevens, at P.O. Box 1, Wallsend Shipyard, Wallsend, and marked Boys' Club Fund.

All local firms are to be asked for support and, although many already contribute regularly, it is expected that they will rally round to make this extra effort.

The club—now holding normal activities as far as possible in parts of the club premises—also has plans for raising some of the money.

"We have 12 months to raise the money," said its leader, Mr. Frank Herdman. "It is an ambitious plan but we feel justified in making the appeal because ultimately every part of the town benefits by getting a better citizen morally, mentally and physically."

W. News 19 6 59

Wallsend News Friday 19th June 1959.

Chapter 6 – The end of one club and the beginning of another

A t the time of the 1959 fire Wallsend Boys' Club already had a reputation in the town for its range of activities and for success. Among the trophies that survived the blaze by being stored in a fire-proof safe were Northumberland County Senior and Junior Boxing Championship trophies, the YOC League Challenge cup for football, and the Milburn Cup for athletics. Not surprisingly therefore, there was a fair amount of support for getting the club going again.

Within eight days of the fire donations worth £70 had been received, unsolicited, as well as £30 worth of goods. The Commanding Officer of the TA, based in Vine Street in Wallsend, called upon the Wallsend News to launch an appeal to get the necessary funds for a new clubhouse.

He referred to the 'yeoman service' which the club provided for the town and pledged £50 from the squadron to get the appeal underway.

In order to build a new brick clubhouse, less susceptible to future fires, it was going to be necessary to raise about £2500 in 12 months. This would then qualify the club for a Ministerial grant of a further £8000.

At the same time, the club committee asked the Town Council to grant a lease for the land for the new club, which would be largely where the old 'wooden hut' had been, but with a slightly extended plot. The Mayor of the town, Councillor Grogan, promised his "whole-hearted support".

From the beginning, the connection with Swan Hunter's was going to be crucial again, with Mr Vic Stevens of the firm being the named person to whom donations should be sent.

All local firms were asked for support and although many already contributed regularly, they rallied round to make an extra effort. Plans were then formulated to raise funds towards the proposed new building

"We have 12 months to raise the money," said Frank Herdman, again quoted in the local press. "It is an ambitious plan but we feel justified in making the appeal because ultimately every part of the town benefits."

In August 1959, a promise from singer Frankie Vaughan had raised hopes in the club. Frank Herdman had written to Frankie Vaughan, a keen Boys' Club supporter, to ask if he could help, but when he discovered that Frankie was appearing at the City Hall, Newcastle, he decided to see him personally. Together with a Wallsend News reporter and a photographer, he visited the singer.

When Frankie heard of the Clubs plight he promised that if he came north to do a tour of the Boys' clubs during Youth Club Week in October, he would definitely come to Wallsend and do a show.

"It would give me great pleasure to do so," said Frankie, who recalled that several boys from the Wallsend Club had appeared with him in his 'Clubs are Trumps' show, which he had done in London the previous year to help raise funds for the youth club movement.

Frankie was not the only performer to be touched by the plight of the club, for Miss Lorne Lesley, a singer appearing in Newcastle with him, was also quoted as promising,

"I will be thrilled and delighted if I can sing with Frankie at your club". Preparations were duly made for the show which Frank Herdman hoped to put on at the club during "Club Week". The majority of performers would be local artists, many of them being amateurs from neighbouring clubs. The takings would go towards the repairing of the clubhouse. Unfortunately, Frankie Vaughan was unable to keep his promise to appear in the Wallsend Boys' Club show. "His commitments in the States kept him there for much longer than he expected", said the press at the time.

"We are naturally disappointed that Frankie will be unable to appear," said Frank Herdman. "We still intend to put on a show though, and at this moment we are running a beauty competition and hoping to start a talent competition".

Each week during the Wednesday night dance at the club, three girls were chosen to appear in a grand final, which was to be held when the club put on a variety show.

The club continued to meet in the undamaged part of the old building and used this as it launched its own fund-raising efforts.

As it became clear that there was a will that the club should survive, serious thought was given as to what the new building should look like. Should it mimic the old one, though made of brick instead of wood?

It was recognised by many that times had changed dramatically over the twenty years since the first club was opened, and so had the interests of young people. There hadn't been a pantomime in WBC for several years, and didn't seem to be the same interest in theatrical pursuits, so a stage seemed redundant. Even boxing, which had been so popular in the club, seemed to have temporarily fallen out of favour.

Wallsend boys for Frankie Vaughan show

Members of Wallsend Boys' Club have been chosen to take part in the annual Frankie Vaughan Boys' Club show at the Royal Festival Hall, London, on Monday week—the first youths from Wallsend ever to do so.

They are the Red Planets skiffle group and comedian John White aged 20 a miner of Ryton Gardens, Howdon. The show will be televised.

John has a ten-minute solo spot and the Red Planets will accompany Frankie in a song.

This is the first time that anyone has been chosen for the show north of Birmingham.

Wallsend News
11th October 1958.

Disappointment

Singer Frankie Vaughan will be unable to keep his promise to appear in a Wallsend Boys Club show. "His commitments in the States will keep him there for much longer than he expected." club leader Frank Herdman told me.

Frank saw the singer when he appeared in Newcastle a few weeks ago, and told him of the club's need for funds since their premises were burnt out in a fire earlier in the year. Frankie Vaughan, who was due to make a tour of several clubs in the North-east, promised that the Wallsend club would go to the top of the list.

"We are naturally disappointed that Frankie will be unable to appear." said Mr. Herdman. "We still intend to put on a show though, and at this moment we are running a beauty competition and hoping to start a talent competition."

Each week, during the Wednesday night dance at the club three pretty girls will be chosen to appear in a grand final which will be held when the club puts on a variety show "in the not too distant future".

"The only stipulation for entries in the beauty competition is that the girls must have been to three club functions." Mr. Herdman told me.

Other plans for helping the club to raise funds for the re-decoration of the clubhouse include another talent competition which will be held in a local cinema. Winners of this will also appear in the bumper variety show.

Wallsend News 23rd October 1959.

According to J. McNally's essay, the main interests of the late 1950s were felt to be 5-a-side football, judo and basketball.

Without taking away any possibility of a later resurgence of interest in activities like boxing, it was felt that the new building should be as flexible in design as possible, and that something more open plan than the old 'L' shaped 'wooden hut' would be appropriate. Another factor which came into the equation was that the Northumberland Association of Boys' Clubs had no premises big enough to host County activities. In order to arrange these functions they had to hire halls around the county with all the attendant cost. The rebuilding of Wallsend Boys' Club offered the possibility of remedying this situation.

As in the 1930s, one of the driving forces behind the birth of the new club was the man who had been President since 1938, Mr Sheriton Clements Swan, one of the directors of Swan Hunter and Wigham Richardson's. Mr Swan was heavily involved in the process of getting planning permission and drawing up plans for the new club. The first application was ready in November 1959, less than six months since the fire. During 1960, as the interest of the Northumberland Association of Boys' Clubs grew, so the plans were amended and developed.

As another sign of the changing times, the local council were concerned that there should be plenty of car parking facilities on the club premises and that access by car should be safe and regulated. In spite of such a prompt start to planning and fund raising, the process of waiting for permission to build the new club, for agreements over the lease of the land, and then of waiting for government grants to become available, was a slow one, as seen from the correspondence described below.

An application for planning permission to build a new clubhouse, to Northumberland County Council, in 1960 had this positive reply:

To Wallsend Borough Council.

"In pursuance of their powers under the above mentioned Act the Northumberland County Council hereby permit the carrying out of the following development: -
   The erection of a Boys' Club at Station Road, Wallsend, in accordance with amended plan, as described in your application for planning permission dated 17th Nov. 1959."

This positive reply from Northumberland County Council initiated this statement to the press from Wallsend Borough Council:

From John Stoker, Solicitor, Wallsend Town Clerk.

"Wallsend Boys' Club may soon become the headquarters for boys' club events of the county status. Plans have been drawn up for a club to replace the one damaged by fire over a year ago. A centre as well equipped and up to date as any in the country is planned.
   Mr C.S. Swan, who is honorary president of the Wallsend Boys' Club explained how the new club would be operated if the plans are accepted.
   The County Association has no boys' clubs suitable for staging county events. Seeing that it is important that we should rebuild the Wallsend Boys' Club, we

feel that this is the opportunity for us to produce a club that will cope with the town's needs with the extra space required for events covering a wider area.

Mr Swan, who has played an important role in the drawing up of the plans, is a director of Swan Hunter and Wigham Richardson's Ltd, Wallsend Shipyard, a firm that has always had an interest in and given support to the club.

He said that at the moment the County Association had to borrow premises in order to stage many events.

Mr Frank Herdman, who has been associated with the club since it first started more than 20 years ago and who has been club leader for the past five years said that if it received approval it would be a wonderful plan for the club, one of the oldest established in the country.

If the development is carried out, members will be able to enjoy modern facilities and equipment.

The present club is a wooden building. One wing was badly damaged by the fire, which swept through it in June 1959, and since then members have worked hard trying to replace the equipment lost in the fire but they are still working under a handicap. "The premises flood when it rains and during the winter it is hard trying to get the lighting and heating to work". Because of this many of the club activities have had to be held outdoors."

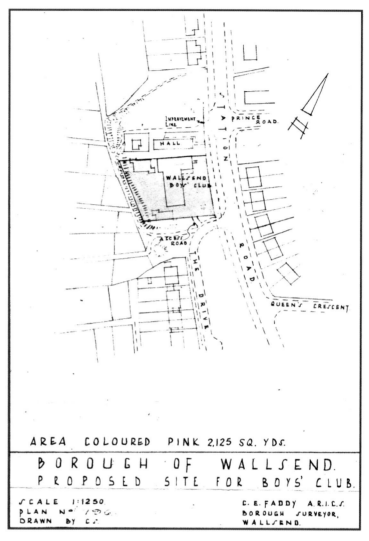

Outline plan for proposed site of new Wallsend Boys' Club.

In 1961 another letter from the Borough Council read as follows:

"I have received the District Valuer's report with reference to the lease of the site, which will be submitted to the next meeting of the Housing and town Planning Committee to be held on the 19th instant. I have also received a letter, dated the 7th instant, from the Clerk of the Northumberland County Council, stating that he has been informed by the Ministry of Housing and Local Government that the Department raises no objections to the Borough Councils proposals to remove the air raid shelters from the site."

From John Stoker, Solicitor, Wallsend Town Clerk.

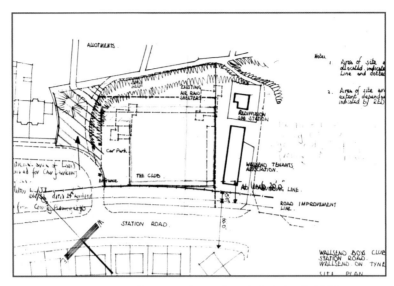

Detailed plan of proposed new boys' club April 1961.

Harold Warfe the architect of the proposed new building sent the following letter to the Boys' club committee in the summer of 1961:

"I have now received official notification of Town Planning and Byelaw approval of our proposals for the above new building. In this respect therefore we are free to proceed to the next stage, although the production of working drawings is being held in abeyance until we hear from the Ministry of Education, but to avoid undue delay when we wish to start building I am developing these in draft outline now, largely for my own satisfaction."

In August 1961 youth club workers throughout the county and particularly in Wallsend waited anxiously to learn the fate of plans submitted for national approval concerning the rebuilding of the Wallsend Boys' Club.

Mr E. Roberts, the organising secretary of the Northumberland Association of Boys' Clubs, mentioned that a reply to the submitted plans was expected by August 1961. Full details of the new club, were yet to be made public, but it was known that the cost would be around £35,000 and the premises would be well equipped and as up to date as any other in the country. The club would then certainly become the headquarters for the Boys' club events of County status, for at that time, the County Association had no suitable facilities. "All we can do is sit tight and wait for a verdict," said Mr Roberts.

Anxious wait

YOUTH club workers throughout the county and particularly in Wallsend are waiting anxiously to learn the fate of plans submitted for national approval concerning the re-building of the Wallsend Boys' Club, which was severely gutted by fire two years ago.

Mr. E. Roberts, the organising secretary of the Northumberland Association of Boys' Clubs, told me this week that a reply to the submitted plans is expected within the next month.

Full details of the new club —should building permission be granted—have yet to be made public, but it is known that the cost would be around £35,000 and the premises would be as well equipped and up to date as any other in the country.

The club would then certainly become the headquarters for boys' club events of county status, for to date the County Association has no suitable facilities.

"All we can do is to sit tight and wait for a verdict," said Mr. Roberts.

25·8·61

Wallsend News 25th August 1961.

In September 1961 the Boys' Club Committee had to instruct their solicitors Dickinson, Miller and Turnbull to write the following letter to Wallsend Borough Council regarding the high rent proposed for the new Boys' Club site:

"I thank you for your letter of the 15th instant, enclosing a copy of the lease from the Town Clerk of Wallsend and, quite frankly I am not at all happy about this.

This is a ninety nine years lease at a rent of £100 per annum which is a pretty substantial commitment and the Boys' Club commit themselves purely to use the premises as a non profit making Boys' Club, I do not think that one can possibly commit oneself in a lease of this nature to use the premises for this purpose during the next ninety nine years.

The Boys' Club are presumably going to spend a considerable sum of money on the new premises and if, for any reason at all, the Boys' Club is closed, they would naturally wish to try to obtain back some of their expenditure by selling the premises and this will certainly not be possible with this restriction.

Apart from the above, the draft lease is satisfactory."
                                    Yours Sincerely

         I.J.Dickinson

The letter to the council fell on deaf ears with no positive response from them.

In 1962 with funding from the government not forthcoming, the council reviewed their proposed rental as the following letter shows:

"In view of the fact that the Ministry are not prepared to give grant aid to the Boys' Club at the present time Wallsend Council have agreed that we can continue to lease the building on the present basis namely £1 per annum until next March, when the matter can again be reviewed. This is indeed most satisfactory. I take it that we will not now sign the new lease until next year."

Since September 1960 the club had only been opening 3 nights a week, on Tuesdays, Wednesdays, and Thursdays, and membership had dropped to about 50. The premises flooded when it rained, and lighting and heating often didn't work well in winter. As a result, most of the club activities were planned for outdoors. It was to take until July 1964 before grant aid was obtained from the Ministry of Education and Science and progress could be made, and then took another

Another blaze at boys' club

WALLSEND Boys' Club, Station Road, was on fire again this week, for the third time.

People on their way to work on Tuesday morning noticed the fire and called the brigade. The almost gutted building was completely destroyed by the fire, which took Wallsend Fire Brigade nearly an hour to get under control. Firemen were dampening down the smouldering remains for some time afterwards.

The building was seriously damaged by a fire about four years ago which wrecked one wing of the building, and about four weeks ago fire broke out again, causing more damage.

There was very little in the building on Tuesday, except an old piano and a few pieces of gymnastic equipment. Fortunately, the Fire Brigade was able to prevent the blaze spreading to the wooden headquarters of the High Farm Residents' Association nearby.

Wallsend News 1st November 1963.

year for work to commence. This was not a moment too soon, because by then the remains of the premises had been completely destroyed by two more fires.

The first of these was at the beginning of October 1963 and caused substantial damage and almost gutted the building. Then on November 1st 1963 came the third fire which completely destroyed everything that remained. Only the prompt actions of the Fire Brigade stopped the fire spreading to the nearby High Farm Residents Association hut. The press reported that it took Wallsend Fire Brigade almost an hour to get the fire under control. By the time of this final fire there was very little left in the building other than what the press described as "an old piano" (presumably the very piano which had accompanied all those pantos and shows) and a few pieces of gymnastic equipment.

So disappeared the last remnants of the original Wallsend Boys' Club.

On 14th July 1964. Wallsend Boys' Club were pleased to hear from the Boys' Club Association that the necessary award of grant aid from the Ministry had now been obtained and that the construction of the new Club would now proceed and they were accordingly getting in touch with Wallsend Corporation to finalise the negotiations for the lease.

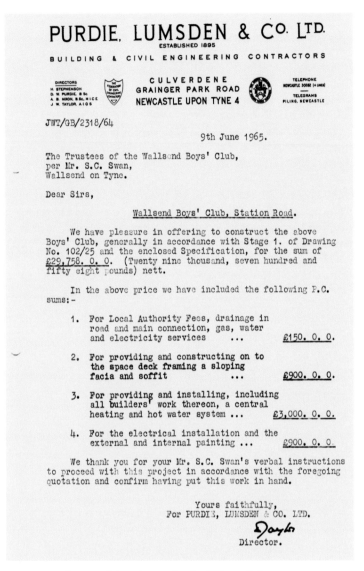

Successful estimate for building of the new Wallsend Boys' Club.

On 6th November Northumberland County Council approved a grant of £6,875, which was recommended by Northumberland Education Committee towards the cost of erecting premises for Wallsend Boys' Club.

On 11th June 1965 Purdie, Lumsden & Co, Ltd won the contract to build the new Wallsend Boys' Club, and sent a letter thanking the committee for accepting their tender.

The planned new building was 90 feet square by 30 feet high and was made up of three tiers, or decks as they became known, keeping up the shipbuilding connection. As described in some detail by J. McNally, the lower deck was to be the main sports hall, ninety feet long and fifty feet wide with a wooden floor made of maple and white block brick walls leading to panelling above and opaque glass at ceiling level. Four feet above the sports floor would be the Middle deck which could be used for spectators or curtained off to make a stage for dramatics or concerts.

Also at this level would be the reception hall, leader's office, toilets and changing facilities with showers and three small rooms for crafts, meetings, and a quiet room.

The horse shoe shaped Upper deck provided space for billiards, table tennis, darts and a canteen. There would also be more room for spectators here. This area and the Middle deck would be surrounded by railings.

The builders, Purdie Lumsden of Newcastle, were engaged to erect the building and they decided it should be done in three stages, with the main shell being erected first. The second phase would be the making of a Car Park leading up to the main entrance and a garden at the front, all surrounded by a low perimeter wall. The third phase was to consist of installing a suspended ceiling with recessed lighting to camouflage the steel work in the flat roof. It was anticipated that this work would take two years in total. Because the cost of the first two phases exceeded estimates by £6000, the third phase was never really completed. By the time the building was completed, the final cost was about £38,590.

Much of the indoor work on the building was completed by workers from Swan Hunters, another gift from Sheriton C. Swan. This contributed a rather nautical feel to the building, with ships' stair cases being erected to link the 'decks'.

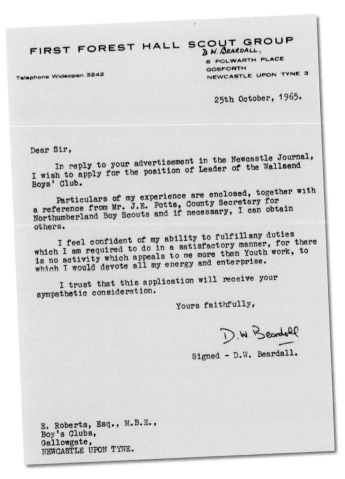

David Beardall's application letter for the Wallsend Boys' Club Leaders job.

In December 1965 the club committee appointed a new full-time leader for Wallsend Boys' Club, 28 year old Dave Beardall. The interviews for the appointment took place at Swan Hunter's since the club building was incomplete. Once appointed the new club leader, along with Wally Telfer who was Development Officer for the NABC, had the task of spending a grant of £2500 allocated by the Department of Education and Science on equipment and furnishings.

Among the equipment bought early on were a full-size judo mat and cover, boxing equipment, a trampoline, three table tennis tables, nets and bats. Furnishings such as tables, chairs, desks and curtains were also acquired.

Wallsend Boys' Club

President : S. C. SWAN
Chairman : D. LEETE

Hon. Treasurer and Secretary :
V. STEVENS
Wallsend Shipyard
Wallsend-on-Tyne
Telephone 6-3121

Club Leader :
F. J. HERDMAN

STATION ROAD
WALLSEND-ON-TYNE

3rd December, 1965.

D.W. Beardall, Esq.,
8, Polwarth Place,
Gosforth,
NEWCASTLE UPON TYNE 3.

Dear Mr. Beardall,

With reference to your interview this morning, and for the purpose of record, I confirm the decision of the Committee to appoint you as full time Club Leader of this Club. The appointment to take effect as from 16th December 1965. As arranged you will negotiate with Mr. McGlynn of the Northumberland Education Committee the appropriate salary for this appointment.

I trust that you will have every success in this position, and I look forward to our association in this work.

Yours sincerely,

David Beardall's letter of appointment as Leader of the new Wallsend Boys' Club.

Wallsend Boys' Club under construction.

By May 1966 the club was able to unofficially open for business, though still not completely finished off. After the years in abeyance it was probably not surprising that there were only twenty boys in attendance on that first night. But the club soon built up a momentum again, not least because the facilities were far ahead of those of any other club of its type. By the end of the month there were enough members to start a judo class led by George Oughton. This in turn attracted more boys, and enrolment for membership opened on June 1st 1966. Applicants had to be between the ages of 14 and 21. By July 1966 the club had 200 members and Dave Beardall was quoted in the local press as saying that everything was "proceeding very satisfactorily." One of the particularly memorable events to take place in that month was a gathering of club members and leaders on July 30th to watch England win the world cup around a borrowed TV set in the club.

Young David Beardall.

During these first weeks a committee of club members was formed, one of whose first challenges – and an on-going one – was to raise funds for the club.

Their first planned venture was a charity cricket match between the cast of 'My Fair Lady', which was being staged at the Theatre Royal in Newcastle, and a Mayor of Wallsend's eleven. Which included members of Newcastle United football team.

The 'My Fair Lady' cast included Tony Britton, Wendy Bowman, Bert Brownbill, Patrick Waddington, Gwynne Whitby and Gavin Gordon, all of whom signed a commemorative programme.

The game was to be staged on July 31st 1966 at Bigges Main, but plans to charge 1/- admittance fee had to be scrapped because of the Lord's Day Observance Act since July 31st was a Sunday. As a result a collection was taken at the match instead, resulting in rather less revenue than had been hoped for.

The theme of fund raising was one which was to appear repeatedly in the decades ahead, and indeed still does. Grants were, and are, variable and unreliable sources of funding, so fund raising events were always needed. This applied to all Boys' Clubs of course, so one week a year was designated 'Boys' Club week' and permission was given for house-to-house collections etc.

David Beardall, was delighted with the response of the people of Wallsend in the house-to-house collection made in Boys' Club Week in that first November of the new club.

He was quoted in the Wallsend News as saying: "Club members collected £184.10s which was particularly praiseworthy in the view of the fact that the club has been in operation only a short time".

All Star Cricket Match!

Mayor of Wallsend XI v My Fair Lady XI

Newcastle United Footballers   Tony Britton, Cast of
                                My Fair Lady
                                TV Personalities

Sunday 31 July 1966
2.15 pm

Bigges Main, Wallsend

Refreshments   Admission ½/-

Dave thanked the Town for their cooperation.

Dave also expressed appreciation of the £20 raised by Mr Norman Wright, manager of the Boro Bingo, on the corner of Park Road and the High Street, after he had a collection amongst his club members for the Boys' Club.

By this stage, preparations were well underway for the official opening of Wallsend Boys' Club in its new building. Dave Beardall was keen to extend an invitation to all former members of the club but was hampered by the loss of all club records in the fires.

He used the local press therefore to advertise the opening on December 16th.

Chapter 7 – Phoenix from the ashes: Wallsend Boys' Club rises again

The opening ceremony of what was described as "the best club building in the North of England" (Duke of Northumberland in his opening speech) had many links with the opening of the old wooden hut in 1938. Sheriton Clements Swan was still present as club president - a remarkable sign of commitment – and he welcomed the Duke of Northumberland to carry out the official opening, reminding the 150 people present that it was the Duke's mother, when Duchess of Northumberland, who had carried out that first opening ceremony.

In his speech, the Duke spoke warmly of the role Wallsend Boys' Club had played in the community of Wallsend since 1938. He paid particular tribute to Mr Swan, pointing out that, "Without him, the club could not have achieved so much." The Mayor of Wallsend, Councillor R. Fleming, also praised the work of Sheriton Swan, saying that through him, "Wallsend Boys' Club has become part of the great social scheme of Swan Hunter's shipyard, and it is an asset to the town."

The Duke of Northumberland was presented with a tie bearing the new emblem of Wallsend Boys' Club, a swan, referring of course to the close links to Swan Hunter's. This presentation was carried out by the chairman of the Boys' committee, Alan Connolly. The Duke immediately put on his new tie, giving Alan his own tie in return.

Mr Swan was also presented with a tie by Martin Adams, another member of the Boys' committee.

Among the other dignitaries and guests who received ties were Lord Ridley, Vice Chairman of the NABC, Mr P. McGlyn, Chief Youth Officer of the Northumberland Education Committee, and Mr Vic Stevens, Secretary and Treasurer of the club's management committee as well as company secretary at Swan Hunter's.

As part of the opening ceremony the Management Committee expressed their thanks to all the following in connection with the building of Wallsend Boys' Club.

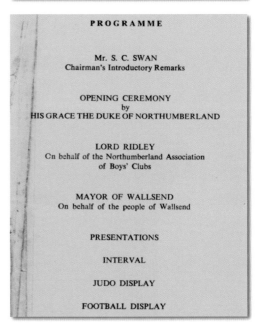

Official Opening of The Wallsend Boys' Club

by

His Grace the Duke of Northumberland K.G.

16 December 1966

PROGRAMME

Mr. S. C. SWAN
Chairman's Introductory Remarks

OPENING CEREMONY
by
HIS GRACE THE DUKE OF NORTHUMBERLAND

LORD RIDLEY
On behalf of the Northumberland Association
of Boys' Clubs

MAYOR OF WALLSEND
On behalf of the people of Wallsend

PRESENTATIONS

INTERVAL

JUDO DISPLAY

FOOTBALL DISPLAY

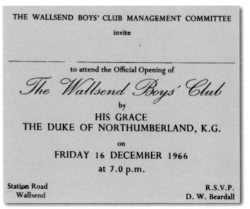

THE WALLSEND BOYS' CLUB MANAGEMENT COMMITTEE
invite

to attend the Official Opening of

The Wallsend Boys' Club
by
HIS GRACE
THE DUKE OF NORTHUMBERLAND, K.G.
on
FRIDAY 16 DECEMBER 1966
at 7.0 p.m.

Station Road
Wallsend

R.S.V.P.
D. W. Beardall

Purdie Lumsden & Co. Ltd, main contractors, Denings Ltd, Rutheroid Co. Ltd, site Contractors Ltd, Swarland Brick Co. Ltd, Thermalite Young Ltd, Samuel Tyzack & Co. Ltd, G.W. Dixon Ltd, Durasic Ltd, Hewetsons, J.T.Leake & Co. Ltd, Rowell's (1924) Ltd, John Porter Ltd, N.F.Ramsey & Co. Ltd, Newcastle Glazing Co. Ltd, A & B Printers Ltd, Henry Hope & Son Ltd and General Concrete Products Ltd.

New club tie tribute to their president
A SWAN CARRIES THE THANKS OF 170 BOYS

Wallsend News December 1966.

Official opening of Wallsend Boys' Club. Friday 16th December 1966. Duke of Northumberland receiving Wallsend Boys' Club tie from Chairman of the boys committee Alan Connolly.

After the speeches and presentations there was a display of judo and football by club members. The club was now officially open for business and a pattern was set early on of involvement in a range of activities which certainly became dominated by football, but never to the exclusion of everything else.

In August 1966 the club had one football team, the under 16s.

Under 16's 1966/7 Season.

Links were being formed with other associations near and far. No sooner was the club opened than, on December 31st, a group of footballers travelled 150 miles to Perth for a match against Perth City Boys' club.

They travelled by mini bus and slept in the Perth club house in sleeping bags the night before the game.

In spite of 'roughing it' a bit, Wallsend Boys' Club team still won 3 – 1.

In April 1967 the Perth boys reciprocated, staying for two nights in the club house. On the Saturday they all went to St James' Park with some of their hosts to see Newcastle United play West Ham. On the Sunday they played a return match at the Rising Sun ground. The result of the match is not recorded. Their comment in the WBC visitors' book states: "This is a lovely club of which we are most envious".

Perth Trip.

Early in 1967 the club received a letter from King George's Jubilee Trust, St. James's Palace, London.

"I was most impressed with the very fine premises you have now got with the help and interest of Swan Hunter & Co., and I am sure that you will make very good use of the facilities provided.

I also hope that your endeavour to get the Duke of Edinburgh's Award Scheme started will be successful, as I am sure it will".

Perth City Boys' club were not the only visitors to come to WBC that year. In March Arthur Horsfield, who had played as centre forward for both Middlesbrough and Newcastle, visited the club and signed the visitors' book. Bennett's End YC from Hemel Hempstead and Frentford Boys' Club from Ilford, also visited in the same month, and indicated that they had enjoyed their stay.

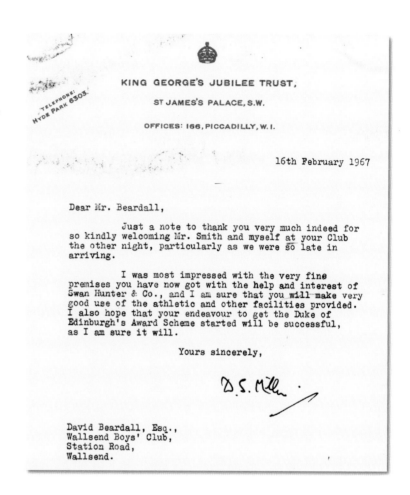

In April, as a fund raising event, a Ball was held in the Club. Five hundred tickets were printed at a cost of £2.2s. Other costs included the following:

To hire Sound Reproducing Equipment, from Mortonsound, (Specialists in Sound Recording Equipment, Oxford St. Newcastle) this included installation and subsequent dismantling for the function - £4.4s.

Band for the night - £30 (no record of who the band was)

Piano Deposit - £10.

Drinks for guests - £14.7s. Feren's Transport, which transported furniture etc from Newcastle Breweries, Scout Headquarters, Osborne Road, Forest Hall to the Boys' Club and back for a cost of £10.10s.

In spite of these expenses, the profit for the night was £39.15.11.

Some of the guests who attended the function were Purdie Lumsden (Contractor), Dick Fleming (Mayor of Wallsend), Jonathan Burton (Lord Mayor of Newcastle), Una Burton (Lady Mayoress of Newcastle), Robert Meadows (Mayor of Tynemouth), Nora Meadows (Mayoress of Tynemouth), John Wheatly (Mayor of Gateshead), L. Wheatly (Mayoress of Gateshead) and members of the Rotary Club, Wallsend.

This was followed up in May by a 'Guess the Goal' competition. In this, competitors had to guess the time of the first goal in the 1967 F.A. Cup Final between Tottenham and Chelsea. This was judged by Mr Albert Stubbins, Sports Reporter for the "Wallsend News". With the aid of a stopwatch he gave the exact time of the goal, and the result of the competition was given in the following week's "Wallsend News". The winner received £10, and there were five consolation prizes. In the event that no one guessed the correct time, the competitor who was nearest was judged the winner. Tickets cost a

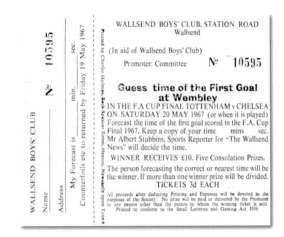

huge 3d each. There seems to be no record of who the lucky winner was, but the event added a bit more to the WBC finances.

To round off the football season a presentation night, including dinner, was held in the club in June and Dave Hilley, who played inside right for Newcastle, attended and presented trophies. David Beardall congratulated members of the football teams on their enthusiasm throughout the season.

Among those who received recognition was Alan Dodds, captain of the junior team. He was honoured as Junior Footballer of the year. Other players who had made regular appearances for the club sides throughout the season were presented with plaques.

In his speech Dave Hilley said, "Many football clubs would be envious of the training facilities at the club, and the premises are excellent for all kinds of sport." Presentations were made to senior boys, B. Ward, G. Reay, D. Graham, D. Wadington and J. Montgomery.

Albert Stubbins.

Presentations were made to junior boys, G. McBlain, D. Wells, F. Hunter, R. Walters, A. Pittam, A. Dodd's, G. Gilchrist, I. Ricalton and F. Blain. After the dinner and presentations the boys watched a film of the famous 1960 European cup final between Entracht and Real Madrid.

The club year ended in July with a visit from the sports reporter for the Wallsend News, Albert Stubbins, which was by no means the last evidence of journalistic interest in the Boys' Club. In fact the following January the Football Pink, the regional football weekly, declared Wallsend Boys' Club to be the team of the month for outstanding football performances during that month.

The summer of 1967 also marked the exit of Dave Beardall for a year, since he went on a Youth Leadership course at Leicester. In his absence, the club was led by Brian Nicholson. Visitors continued to come to the club.

Evening Chronicle Football Pink

TEAM OF THE MONTH AWARD

Wallsend Boys' Club   WAS AWARDED   *High Commendation*
FOR OUTSTANDING SOCCER PERFORMANCE DURING   *January 1968*

Signed   EDITOR

The final event of the year 1967 came just before Christmas, when Pudsey juniors from Leeds visited the Boys' club for a weekend.

In April 1968 it was the turn of Charleston Boys' Club and Douglas Park Boys' Club from Dundee. They seem to have been very impressed by their trip, describing it in the visitors' book as "immense, brilliant, excellent" and remarking on how well fed they had been!

This was followed up in June by a visit from a Mr Stanley Smith of Chelsea Boys' Club.

Other amateur football clubs such as South Shields began to use the club facilities for training sessions.

In spite of all these visitors, and the favourable attention which the club received from the press, there was an ongoing struggle to make ends meet financially.

It seemed as the years went on that the two themes of footballing fame and the need to raise money to keep the club going were constant features of club life. In November 1968, in an effort to attract more young people into the club, one of the workshops on the premises was turned into a 'discotheque' and a Club Week Dance was held with "soft lights and sweet music" to quote the local paper. This was from 8pm until midnight and there was a buffet, spot prizes and a cabaret. The tickets cost 7/6 (37.5 pence today) and this included refreshments.

The Wallsend News reported the event as follows:

When boy wants to meet girl.
Soft lights and sweet music, hardly what you would expect to find in a Boys' club, but this is what Wallsend Boys' Club had in mind. The idea was to let the local girls come in from the cold. A large room that was being used as a workshop was to be turned into a discothèque, with soft ultra violet lights and music to which members could bring their girlfriends. "Since the new club opened there have been several complaints from various quarters that while things were looking up for the boys there were precious little locally for the girls" said David Beardall, the Club

Leader. "The Club Committee, the Management Committee and I agree the complaints were justified, so we decided to give things a trial".

"When we get the room ready we will allow the girls in two nights a week, and if the venture is a success they will probably be admitted to full membership".

The name of the club however would still remain Wallsend Boys' Club added Mr Beardall. As a sideline in his club leadership Dave Beardall hoped to be able to help the local Youth Employment Officer with information on careers for members. Appealing for public support for the club Dave said that during the time that he had worked there he felt there were many people in the town who were interested in youth work but were rather shy about coming forward to help. "They seem to think that a full-time leader can achieve everything, this is far from the case. I need all the help possible from parents and friends.

The N.A.B.C International Boxing Championships were held at the boys club in March 1969 Under A.B.A rules.

Although, as is evident from some of these items, the main focus of Wallsend Boys' club was never solely football, it was certainly its success in producing talented footballers which caught the attention of the media at different times from 1965, as is outlined in more detail in the next chapter.

Inevitably there were also strong links with the nearest big professional football club, Newcastle United. This first reached a peak in a particularly memorable way in June 1969 when David Beardall drove a full coach of club members all the way to Budapest in Hungary to watch their heroes from United beat Ujpest Dozsa in the European Inter City Fairs' Cup Final.

David Beardall with Wallsend Boys' Club members on trip to Ujpest Dozsa 1969.

This journey was no mean feat at the time. The Cold War was still going strong and the group set out on their 2,870 mile journey with neither visas nor tickets. Dave recalls how after camping on the first night in Austria they set off for the Hungarian border to find themselves surrounded in no-man's land by heavily armed border guards. On hearing of their planned destination, the guards provided visas and allowed them to continue their journey. It took another three days to reach the ground, where the exhausted party set up camp again. At 5 in the morning an Ujpest official woke them up to provide free tickets and bacon sandwiches. Having watched a game in which Newcastle (3 – 0 up from the home leg) came back from 2 – 0 down to win 3 – 2, the boys ended up in the Newcastle dressing room sharing some of the victory champagne.

The 1960s ended therefore on a strong and positive note for Wallsend Boys' Club. They had come back strongly from near extinction, were establishing good football teams and running other sporting events, and seemed to be having a good time into the bargain. Club week 1969 saw a fund raising event at Forest Hall Unionist Club when a 'Star Cabaret' was held with a Ploughman's Supper included in the 4/- ticket price.

In December 1969 guests at the WBC Christmas party included the Mayor of Wallsend, the Deputy Mayor and Deputy Mayoress, and Stan Ternant and Derek Foster from Sunderland F.C.

One break from the past also came at this time however, when Sheriton C. Swan, President for 30 years since the club was opened, resigned from that position for personal reasons. His place as president was taken by one of the original club members from 1938, James McBlain. Jimmy had originally left the club in the mid-1940s when he was called up into the armed forces. On his return he had kept up an interest in the club and in 1966 was elected onto the management committee where he served for three years. Mr Swan's resignation saw Jimmy elected President, a position he held until his own resignation in 1976.

Star Cabaret

ON FRIDAY 24th OCTOBER 1969

FOREST HALL CONSTITUTIONAL & UNIONIST CLUB

Doors Open 7.30 p.m.

4s 0d . PRICE INCLUDES PLOUGHMAN'S SUPPER

Vic Stevens with Jimmy McBlain.

Chapter 8 – Football to the Forefront 1969 - 1980

The 1970s were very significant years in the history of Wallsend Boys' Club since it seems to have been that decade in particular that established its strong reputation for turning out first class footballers. On June 19th 1980 an article in the 'Evening Chronicle', written by John Gibson, described Wallsend Boys' club as a breeding ground for football league stars. It pointed out that at that particular moment in time 12 out of a squad of 15 under-15 players were signed up with league clubs. It also listed just some of the professional players of the time who had started their careers at Wallsend Boys' Club. Among them were Ray Hankin, Eric Steele, Alan Waddle, Peter Beardsley, Rob Hindmarch, Mick Tait, Les Taylor, Steve Bruce, Tony Sealy, David Lawson, Gordon Nisbet, Phil Cavanagh, and Ian Watson.

Many of the players listed above were still at very early stages in their careers, and there were other players still to come through the ranks of the WBC teams.

How had this come about? Clearly there had never been a deliberate decision made to make football the particular focus of excellence of the club. And it was still by no means the only activity in which the club did well. But clearly something unusual was happening at the club judging by the sheer quantity and quality of the players being produced there.

That 1980 newspaper article gave a lot of the credit to one man, Peter Kirkley, who had joined the club in 1969 as footballing coach. At that time, just as the club had established itself into its new premises, Dave Beardall recognised that he needed help to run the footballing side of things and persuaded a local football coach, Peter Kirkley, who was already working with teams of young players in the other end of the borough, to join him at WBC. Peter then took over the running of the eleven-a-side football teams.

Young Peter Kirkley.

When he took over there was only one such team, but this was soon to change. By the time the 1980 article was written, there were seven, all with their own manager.

Peter, who was also assistant manager at the Wallsend Sports Centre, was proud of the fact that all his league stars were local. Players had to live within a five-mile radius of the Boys' Club, but the majority came from within two miles of the Club.

Years later Peter Kirkley was to say that he was interested not just in the potential stars, of whom there were many, but in every boy playing for the club teams. The key was discipline. On turning up for their first coaching session, the boys had to memorise a list of rules which governed things like the subs they had to pay, the smartness of their kit, their punctuality and courtesy, and their behaviour generally, both on and off the pitch. These rules were very much in the tradition of the original Boys' club constitution with its emphasis on supporting the 'mental, physical and social' development of the members. This is one of the repeated themes of the club's progress, the emphasis, which is still current, on good behaviour and good citizenship. The rules also applied to parents on the touchline with parents being encouraged not to get too carried away in encouraging their offspring.

Apart from Peter Kirkley, the football teams over the years have relied, and still rely, on an army of volunteer scouts, managers, and coaches. As the years went by the club made sure that all the coaches were FA trained to add to the professionalism of the club. The early foundations of success were laid not just by Peter but also by men like Sid Sharp who was constantly on the watch for talent. Another example was Bob Slone who ran coaching sessions for the five-a-side teams for 35 years from the late 1960s. This sort of faithful voluntary commitment is what created the conditions for success in the club's football reputation.

Sid Sharp.

One of the first really successful football 'graduates' of WBC of the post-1960s era was Ray Hankin who signed as an apprentice for Burnley at the age of 15 in 1970. After a career playing for several clubs, including Leeds United, Ray then became Football in the Community Manager for Newcastle United.

A newspaper article "Days of real blood and thunder" published in October 1990 in the Evening Chronicle told Ray's story.

"Ray Hankin, an early product of Wallsend Boys' Club, signed as an apprentice for Burnley at the age of 15 in 1970. Ray is now Newcastle United's, Football in the Community Officer, and tells of his colourful career as a player and how its third time lucky at Newcastle.

Bob Slone.

It was a sight to strike fear into the bones of every living man, enough to bring the walls of Jericho tumbling down in submission. The last time there had been an aerial bombardment like it was during the Second World War. Joe Jordan and Ray Hankin were the twin strikers of Leeds United and the rest of football shuddered at the thought of Saturday afternoon, such was their physical presence. "Oh, we caused some damage", said Ray, with a relish, which wiped away the passing years. "Joe was awesome-frightening really. All we did was get the ball in the box and he'd wipe out three or four defenders. In that season of 1977, I scored 21 league goals, a record, which stood at Leeds until Lee Chapman beat it. I just picked up the pieces from the chaos that big Joe caused. We had two wingers in Arthur Graham and Carl Harris, who could catch pigeons and all they did was get the ball in the box, then Joe and I took over."

Joe also played for Manchester United, Scotland and in Serie A, while Ray paraded in the old first division for a magnificent Burnley side at the tender age of 17 and won five England Under-23 caps.

Joe never got the credit for all his all round ability because he was so physically intimidating. He was also quick, excellent in the air and had good technique.

Ray, an early product of the Wallsend Boys' Club production line, never won a full England cap; this was largely due to the fact that throughout his career he was plagued by persistent knee trouble caused by his prodigious leaping off that particular leg. The wear and tear in days when medical science hadn't advanced to today's accepted high standards was colossal.

By the time Ray left Burnley for Leeds United in 1976 for the princely sum of £200,000, he was already suffering. Two games into a new career, Ray had to submit to the hospital knife and was out of action for six long months. He was never rid of the problem for the rest of his career. On hard surfaces it was hopeless he could hardly run. He played at the very highest level with his knee like a pincushion; He had so many cortisone injections, which were lethal. They got you through a game but after-effects were shocking. However, in his day if you were a big-name player they got you out there the best way they could.

Ray escaped the shipyards of the Tyne, which claimed his father, and brother because, being a man in a boy's body, he had both physique and the ability to inevitably take him into professional football. Ray was only 15 in 1970 when he sighed as an apprentice for Burnley, 16 when he made his debut in the Second Division and 17 when he was a regular top-flight player.

Burnley built a side par excellence on a relentless stream of players from the North East - when Ray joined; their manager was another Geordie, Jimmy Adamson. "I hated him at first", admitted Ray, "but I learned to love him and would have walked through fire for him at the end."

He needed discipline as a kid, not because he was a wild boy off the park but because when he crossed that line something took him over. "I would kick my granny - mind you, Jimmy never got that trait out of me completely! I think I cemented my situation at Burnley early doors. Harry Wilson was a left back from up here that was as hard as nails but I tackled him good and proper and he went down like a bag of cement".

Harry jumped up to bop the young upstart who had dared to do such a thing - Ray was only 15 - but he promptly cracked him one.

It seemed to get Ray respect. Adamson was a magnificent coach who would take individual players after training for one-on-one sessions. "I owed him a lot".

Ray with a memory bank bursting with treasures still insists that Burnley is his club. "We had a wonderful side, top quality players and a real spirit about us. I played for a host of clubs including Leeds United, Middlesbrough, Wolves and Vancouver Whitecaps but Turf Moor is my spiritual home as it was for so many of us from the pits and shipyards of the North East."

Ray's success was followed in the early 1970s by that of Eric Steele, a goalkeeper who played for Newcastle and then for Peterborough before becoming a goalkeeping coach. In 1971, as a schoolboy, Eric Steele played his second international football match for the England Schoolboys X1 against Scotland at Burnley. Eric, who was a pupil at Burnside High School, and a member of Wallsend Boys' Club, played in the England v Wales match at Denbigh, two weeks earlier, which England won 2-0. A press article said that Eric, 17 at the time and studying for his 'A' Levels, hoped that when he left school in the summer he could play professional football for Newcastle United. He wanted to see what his exam results were like first because he also had a chance to go to college to study physical education, but he thought playing professional football would probably be his first choice.

Young Eric (1971).

A couple of years later another newspaper article outlined the problem that Eric's skill and ambition caused Joe Harvey, then Newcastle United manager.

"Three into one won't go. That left Newcastle United manager Joe Harvey with a problem of mathematics and goalkeepers. Newcastle's two goalkeepers, Iam McFaul and Martin Burleigh, had proved the right to First Division status but a new challenger for the green shirt had emerged, Eric Steele, an immensely talented 19 year old goalkeeper who was now ready to stake a claim."

Eric is now first team goalkeeping coach at Derby County

Wallsend Boys' Club continued to have many visitors, more and more of them visiting with football in mind.

In February 1970 Jim Smith from Newcastle United paid a visit to the club, with Dave Elliott and Dave Smith also from Newcastle United visiting the club in the March. Later in the year John McNamee a centre half with Newcastle United made a visit to the club.

In 1971 the club had a visit from Tony Green and Alex Reid, both of whom played football for Newcastle United F.C. Kevin Wilson of Sheffield Wednesday F.C also visited.

In June 1972 Bobby Moncur, the captain of Newcastle United presented a trophy to Mick Tait at the Boys' Club Presentation Night, also in attendance was Tyne Tees Television presenter Roderick Griffiths.

In the spring of 1974 Dave Blakey of Burnley F.C. visited the club, followed in April by the F.A. Cup, brought along to let Boys' Club members take a last look at the trophy before Sunderland F.C. returned it to the Football Association. Sunderland player David Young, who helped with the coaching of the Wallsend club's football teams, loaned the F.A. Cup to the club.

There were hopes that Newcastle United would bring the Cup back to Tyneside, but even if that were not to happen, two other clubs in the semi-finals had ex-Wallsend Boys' Club members in their team, Ray Hankin of Burnley and Alan Waddle of Liverpool.

The club Presentation Night that year, in July, saw four ex-members, now professional footballers, presenting trophies and certificates. These were Ray Hankin again, Mick Tait and Les Taylor of Oxford United, and Kevin Wilson of Sheffield Wednesday.

Mick Tait with Bobby Moncur.

In December 1974 Southampton F.C. used the Boys' Club facilities for a training session before playing Newcastle United at St. James's Park. The same month Hordvick Idrettslag from Norway stayed at Wallsend Boys' Club over the Christmas and New Year period.

In 1975 at the club Presentation night the trophies were presented by Stewart Barrowclough of Newcastle United.

There was special cause for celebration that year since the success of two Wallsend Boys' Club teams in a mini World Cup series organised by the NABC set a record for the competition, which was then only three years old. The under – 18 team, captained by Shaun Green, then an electrician, won the cup for their age group without dropping a point. The under-16 team, captained by Rob Hindmarch, were losing finalists.

Between them the Wallsend Boys' conceded only eight goals and scored forty four. They were playing teams from England, Scotland, Ireland, Canada, Norway, Sweden, Holland, Belgium, France, Denmark and West Germany. Both Shaun Green and Rob Hindmarch went on to have

Ian Watson, Rob Hindmarch, Stewart Barrowclough, Tony Sealy and Steve Scott in front.

careers in football. Rob signed for Sunderland and Shaun forged a career as a soccer coach in the USA helping to found the USA Soccer School of Excellence. His is one of many examples of ex-club members who gained careers through football other than by becoming professional players.

In April 1976 a football team called "SPK Nord" from Haugesund, Norway, stayed at the Boys' Club for a long weekend.

Presentation Night in 1979 saw a very special award made to a young man who was to become a very special player. Bob Corkhill, (brother of Tony Corkhill whose story is told in chapter 5) was by that time a successful businessman based in the Netherlands, though born and bred in Wallsend. He had a long connection with youth football, as his story in his own words relates, and in 1979 had helped to organise an international youth tournament in the Netherlands. One of the competing teams in the tournament, and the eventual winners, were Wallsend Boys' Club. But their diminutive number 10, eighteen year old Peter Beardsley, particularly caught the eye and was voted outstanding player of the tournament. So on that July night in 1979 Bob Corkhill made the journey back to Wallsend to present him with his award.

Bob Corkhill's Story – 'The long and winding road to Peter Beardsley'

Bob Corkhill.

"My trade was plasterer and it would bring me joys and sorrows, and many roads would be travelled to make an honest living."

In the 1950s I headed for Western Germany where extensive war damage brought a demand for building craftsmen. Having played local football around Wallsend, Bigges Main Celtic and Rising Sun FC being two clubs I remember, I decided to join a local German team called Altencelle S.V. With the turmoil of World War II just ended, the football was of a poor nature so I set about giving my best and experience to improve the standards of this village team. Imagine my surprise in later years to be awarded the medal and certificate of honour for services in promotion and help to the Altencelle S.V.

I moved into the Netherlands in early 1970, to the city of Den Haag (The Hague). Apart from earning my living Holland was a hive of football activity, a small country with excellent travel facilities so that the top clubs could be easily reached. I remember meeting Sir Bobby Robson at AZ Alkmaar's stadium, during the era of Mick Mills and Paul Marriner I believe. Ruud Krol was another personality I knew. He played for Ajax and Roma. 'Lady Luck' also destined me to meet Brian Clough outside Schiphol Airport with his Notts Forest team during the European Cup.

I was enjoying the "buzz" and I was 'Dutch contact man' (sort of spy) for the late Harold Shepherdson of Middlesbrough FC. I used to give him my ratings of Heine Otto, who later signed and was successful on Teeside.

The desire to be part of junior football was still burning inside me, so I enrolled as youth leader with Vredenburgh Juniors but I never dreamt of the happy ending which lay before me. Organising an international football tournament was part of my task. We needed approximately 16 teams so I brought in my ex-German team Altencelle S.V., also F.C.Menen from Belguim, and offered my home town Wallsend Boys' Club a place in the line up. Thanks to Mr David Beardall and the committee, the offer was accepted.

Now began the hard work, organising accommodation, travel, etc.

Things were soon sorted out and I went down to Rotterdam Europort and met the Boys' Club team. Their escorts, Peter Kirkley, Sid Sharp and John McNally, followed me in their mini-van to the Hague.

So far, so good.

The big day arrived. First came Feyenoord and Wallsend.

What a result … 2 – 0 to us.

Many rounds were played and I was very impressed with Wallsend's diminutive number 10. Whilst short of a tooth or two, he was not short in footballing skills. The rest is history. Wallsend Boys' Club went on to win the tournament and our mighty midget number 10 was voted most outstanding player.

I flew over with the trophy. The 'long and winding road' had led me back again to my place of birth.

The young Peter Beardsley had brought me the greatest moments of youth football and in later life would justify my judgement by showing his talents and skills on the world stage."

Other presentations were made on the same night in July 1979 by people such as Bob Moncur (who had captained Newcastle United in their Fairs' Cup Victory in 1969 and was now manager of Carlisle United), and Ray Hankin still at Leeds United. Among the other achievements to be celebrated that night was the fact that the under-16 team had won the NABC International Tournament by scoring twenty one goals and conceding only one. As was becoming usual, many ex-club members who were now professional players returned for the occasion. Among them were Ian Watson, Rob Hindmarch and Vince Hutton of Sunderland AFC, Phil Cavener and Mick Wardrobe of Burnley, Steve Baker of Southampton and Steve Bruce of Gillingham. Rob Hindmarch and Steve Bruce were also celebrating gaining under-21 England caps. Young Peter Beardsley was soon to join their ranks as a professional, being signed up by Carlisle United. In 1980 twelve of the Wallsend Boys' Club's under fifteen's football team's fifteen strong squad had signed associate schoolboy forms for league clubs, and to keep pace with demand, at their annual presentation night the club announced that they were going to increase the number of teams in the N.A.B.C. leagues from six to seven the following season with teams ranging from under-12's to under-18's. They also asked the F A for permission to stage a two day international, with teams from Holland, Belgium, Scotland and Liverpool invited to take part.

Having considered all those footballing achievements of the 1970s, it is understandable that media attention should have started to focus on WBC as a nursery for great players – hence that article of June 1980. But the tremendous success in other minority sports the club's boys took part in was less well reported. Nevertheless the boys accumulated a wide variety and large number of trophies from other sports. Among these were the 11 club members who took part in the N.A.B.C. Cross Country Championships at Stoke as part of the County team in 1980.

Proudly displaying their trophies are the Wallsend Junior Cross Country team who won the event at the N.A.B.C. Championships. They are Larry Tully, Michael Jeffells, David Harris and Andrew Scott.

Presentation night in 1980 at the end of the season celebrated the fact that the six club teams that season had won between them nine trophies and had been in seven other cup finals. The esteem in which they were held was reflected in the turn out at that presentation night: Hearts manager Bob Moncur travelled down from Edinburgh to attend and Carlisle United's assistant manager John Pickering motored over from the west with chief scout Brian Watson. Peter Beardsley, who had only left Wallsend less than 12 months earlier, to gain instant success at Brunton Park and a £200,000 price tag said, "Peter Kirkley is unquestionably the man behind the club. His work has helped so many of us. He deserves so much credit".

Peter's full story, including how he eventually came back to Newcastle in 1983 via Vancouver, is told later in this book.

This was by no means the end of the football success story of Wallsend Boys' Club, rather just the first time it had come to the attention of the national press. Many of the players mentioned in this chapter were still at very early stages in their careers, and there were other players still to come through the ranks of the W.B.C. teams.

Chapter 9 - Never just football: other events in the 1970s

Finance had always been an issue for the Boys' Club, as it is for any voluntary organisation.

From re-opening in the mid-60s, as John McNally writes in his essay, the club received an annual grant from the local education authority (which was then Northumberland). This paid for 90% of the leader's salary, heating and lighting, cleaning materials, and half the cost of repairs and new capital equipment. It also paid for the rent of the building while Wallsend Corporation (as was) paid the rates. In spite of this, there were many other bills which could only be met by fund raising efforts and subscriptions.

Equipment such as football strips, table tennis apparatus, badminton rackets and so on, were constantly in need of renewal. Furthermore, the transportation of teams to matches and other incidental costs were rising. One major problem for the club over the years was the fact that it didn't have its own pitches so often had to spend money leasing them.

As a result, raising money continued, as it had in the 1950s, to be a regular activity for the members and the committee. Every October there was a national 'Club Week' in which all Boys' Clubs were allowed to run fund raising activities. This gave rise to some entertaining and imaginative ventures which undoubtedly gave a lot of enjoyment to the members who took part, as well as bringing in the much needed revenue.

In October 1970, (Club Week) William Lisgo, David Johnson, John Graham, David Nesbitt, Kevin Gray, Les Fielder and Harvey Montgomery, all members of Wallsend Boys' Club pushed one of their club mates (The baby, David Jamieson) in a pram 73 miles from Gretna Green to Tynemouth and raised more than £150 for Boys' Club Week. "We have already been given a pram for the job," said club leader Dave Beardall to the local press.

Dave Beardall was on the walk which began at 1pm with a send off at Gretna Green by Mr Tom Passmore, once a centre half for Carlisle United. Throughout the trip the boys averaged six miles an hour, occasionally stepping up to a sharp 15 miles an hour trot downhill, and arrived at Tynemouth beach on time, 24 hours later, to be met by John Craggs and David Young, players from Newcastle United. "The boys went rather slowly for the first mile and then discovered that they had been pushing the pram with the brake on".

After that it was plain sailing and they were two hours ahead of schedule at Brampton, so the boys stopped there for an hour.

When the boys arrived on the outskirts of Newcastle they found that they were to have a police escort through Newcastle and Wallsend and on to Tynemouth. The final incident in the marathon was the "Ducking" in the sea of David Jamieson, the young member who was the passenger in the pram when they reached Tynemouth beach.

Later in that same month another big effort was needed to raise money. This time the boys asked for something harder than the pram push and more lads wanted to take part. It was decided to have a sponsored run.

Marathon Relay

A team from the Wallsend Boys' Club would attempt to run in relays from Wallsend Town Hall to Edinburgh Castle and back in 24 hours. They started at Wallsend Boys' Club at 6pm and went via Station Road, Coast Road, Benton Park Road, Four Lane Ends, Westmoor, Sandy Lane, A1 to Morpeth, Alnwick, Belford, Berwick, Haddington to Edinburgh and returned by the same route.

The distance to be covered was 250 miles. This meant that the boys had to run non-stop for 24 hours. This was a dangerous attempt as most of the running was to be on the main London to Edinburgh road. The aid of the 6th Army Training Regiment was sought and they agreed to help. This turned out to be of great value. The four teams of ten boys took turns to run, making it an all-round effort. The teams reached Edinburgh Castle and a small presentation took place. The queen's own Highland Regiment, who were on duty at the time, presented a plaque of their regiment with the Queen's Coat of Arms to the boys. In return the boys gave the regiment a Club Badge.

After their breather, on went the trek. Time was made up and they arrived back at their destination with forty minutes to spare. The expense of this event was high; having to pay for a bus for the journey, but a handsome profit of £273 was made.

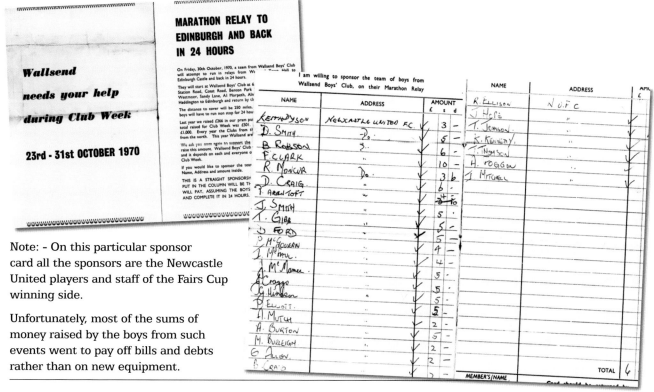

Note: - On this particular sponsor card all the sponsors are the Newcastle United players and staff of the Fairs Cup winning side.

Unfortunately, most of the sums of money raised by the boys from such events went to pay off bills and debts rather than on new equipment.

In spite of financial considerations the club continued to engage in a variety of activities, not just football, and to attract visitors from other clubs. January 1970 had seen the visit of Sedberga Boys' Club from Bradford who stayed at the Boys' Club for the weekend and in August Fairmuir Boys' Club from Dundee, stayed at the Boys' Club for the weekend.

Their comments just before leaving to go home were that the hospitality could not have been better, and they hoped to return in the very near future.

On the 21st of January 1972 Holbeck District Boys' Club stayed at the Boys' Club for a long weekend. On January 26th 1972 the Boys' club held an "At Home" afternoon mainly for the mothers of members. The idea had a double object. Firstly it was not only to let the mothers see where their boys spent their evenings but also to let the women get to know each other. "We felt they might be better able to do this among themselves without their children being there and secondly it would also save our members any embarrassment through having their mothers with them, as would be the case with an evening meeting" said Dave Beardall. He continued, "If as a result of this we can get any of the mothers interested in our activities, all the better. We cannot have too many friends and interested people to help in the running of the Club."

The club premises were also hired out for certain events, which kept it in the public eye as a Wallsend amenity as well as raising money from the hire charges. For example, in October 1973 the Abela-Manning Inter Schools 1st Annual Dance Contest was held at the club with the Mayor and Mayoress of Wallsend in attendance.

In a link to the pre-1959 club, there were still some 'theatrical' activities taking place. In February 1977 Tyne Tees Television filmed part of "The Paper Round Lads". Six members around the age of sixteen were to be used for a fight scene around the table tennis tables. Tyne Tees asked if they could pick out six lads who might make "natural" actors.

Actual filming commenced around 10am and Tyne Tees said they expected to finish all sequences by 5.30-6pm at the very latest.

The final shooting of the above film took place on Wednesday 16th March at North East Marine. 24 members of WBC took part in an eleven-a-side football scene.

One of those lads was Brian Laws, eventually to become manager of Scunthorpe United, Sheffield Wednesday and Burnley. The lads had to be there by 9am. The Director went through certain moves for rehearsal and gave the young actors instructions. The footballers could wear their tracksuits until he gave them the, "We are going for a take" message.

That meant he wanted them to take their tracksuits off and then "give every effort in your acting/footballing capabilities."

Tyne Tees Television gave a donation to the Boys' Club for their assistance.

Wallsend Boys' Club,
Station Road,
Wallsend.
Tyne & Wear.

19th February 1977.

Dear Brian,

     On Wednesday 16th March 1977 Tyne Tees Television require 22 boys to appeaer in episode 7 of the Paper Boy Round. This means getting contracts for you to have permission to be off school.
     Some of you who appeared on Friday 4th of this month do not require the photographs (two) and a medical certificate from your Doctor to say that you are phisicaly fit.
     As the contracts have to be given 21 days notice I would be grateful if you can fill in the form below and return it to me not later than Tuesday 22nd February.

         David Beardall   Leader.

....

I am willing to allow my son (full name) BRIAN LAWS..............

Address..61.WILTSHIRE..GARDENS..WALSEND....TYNE.E.DEAR..

Date of Birth ..14./.10./.61......School..BURNSIDE.HIGH.........

My has not appeared in any/ only once in the same film which is being made called "The Paper Round Boys"

to work as an extra on this film on Wednesday 16th March 1977.

       Signed Mr/Mrs ...E Laws........
               Parent.

Consent form for Brian Laws to appear
in The Paper Round Lads.

Football teams line up for the final scene of The Paper Round Lads.
Brian Laws, middle row, in Newcastle strip, also Colin Shilton, btm row, 5th from the left,
(Now a member of Staff at Wallsend Boys' Club, see page 166) Also in a Newcastle strip.

Filming of The Paper Round Lads at Wallsend Boys' Club 1977.

In July Miss North Tyneside Patricia Morgan paid a visit to the Boys' Club. Later the same year a major fire at the Boys' Club occurred, which cost £15,000 to repair. This was followed a short time later by a huge flood at the club causing more expense and heart ache for the committee, who felt this was a year every one was glad to see the back of.

In July 1980 at the Annual General Meeting of Wallsend Boys' Club, Bob Corkhill (who was living in Holland at the time) was awarded the Honary Life Presidency of the club. The first person to be awarded this honour.

Bob Corkhill 2007 now living back in England.

5th August 1980.

Dear Mr Corkhill,

       At the Annual General Meeting of Wallsend Boys' Club held on Tuesday 15th July it was agreed to offer you Honary Life Vice President of the Club.

       Although I have never met you personally I have spoken to you many times on the telephone, but the work you have done for the visits to Holland have been very good by all accounts.

       I would be grateful if you could let me know if you are willing to become a Life Vice President.

       Hope that you are enjoying the "good" Summer.

       yours sincerely,

David Beardall   Leader.

Mr R. Corkhill,
Van Aalst Lann
238, Zoutermeer.
Holland.

Chapter 10 - The same success: the same old problems 1981-1994

The 1980s and early 1990s saw a continuation of many of the same themes in the life of Wallsend Boys' club.

In January 1981 Joe Harvey and Arthur Cox of Newcastle United visited the club and in March the Boys' Club had a visit from sailors from H M S Sultan, which was moored on the Tyne.

In July 1981 at the annual presentation night, the Club announced an ambitious plan for a 10-day tour of America's east coast the following year. Peter Kirkley unveiled this bold plan before an audience which included a party of Americans over here at the invitation of Wallsend Boys' Club. Others in the audience included League club representatives and former boys' club players who were now making their name in the professional game. The hope was to go over to America with the Under-17 team in June or July 1982, and arrangements had already started.

Wallsend were no strangers to international travel, of course. They had competed in a tournament in Holland for four consecutive years and Bob Corkhill again flew from Amsterdam to make a special presentation at the night in July. Bob's original flight was cancelled and consequently he missed the main presentation but still arrived before the night was over to pay tribute to midfield man Ken Carr. Ken had been voted Wallsend's top player in an Under-18 tournament in Holland, when they finished third behind a Belgian and a German side.

David Beardall, Steve Bruce
and Joe Harvey 1981.

Wallsend Boys' Club ran no fewer than seven teams from Under-12 to Under-18 in 1981 and they won 12 cups during the season that had just ended. Their stature was reflected in the turn out for the presentation of the trophies. Sunderland were represented by new manager Alan Durban, first team coach Mick Docherty, captain Rob Hindmarch, who was a former Wallsend Boys' Club player and commercial manager Corny O' Donnell. Newcastle United had Youth development officer Brian Watson present along with Colin Suggett and Jimmy Nelson.

Among the former Wallsend Boys' who came back for the night were Steve Bruce (Gillingham), Russell Irving (Ipswich), Mark Allen and Geoff Smith (Burnley), and Dave Willis (Newcastle United). Alan Durban, at one of his first public functions as Sunderland boss handed over an England Boys International Cap to Neil McDonald.

Neil McDonald with Alan Durban.

Apart from fund-raising events and football, the club continued to foster interest in other sporting activities. Cross-country running had become another area in which the club excelled. Mike McLeod used to run for W.B.C. long before his success in Olympic and National Cross-country events. In fact, in 1981 when the first ever Great North Run was held, Mike McLeod was the first overall winner.

In March 1982 there was an unusual episode in the history of Wallsend Boys' club when Barnstoneworth United five-a-side team picketed them after their manager was banned when their team was accused of bringing the game into disrepute. Barnstoneworth United knew they were no great shakes in the Wallsend Boys' Clubs under-17's and under-18's five-a-side leagues. They even named

Mike McLeod at W.B.C. presentation night 1981.

their team after a side in television comedy Ripping Yarns. But the players began to take things seriously when they were officially accused of bringing the game into disrepute.

They picketed a league meeting when their player manager was banned and police had to be called in as the row reached fever pitch.

The team – reduced to four players - asked for a reprieve and appealed to get their manager back into the side.

Sixteen-year-old Andrew Bowman of Laburnum Avenue Wallsend, who was the teams top scorer with just three goals to his credit, said "I think it is the fact that we do not mind losing (in fact I think we are quite accomplished losers) that annoys the committee".

"We ARE bad players, in fact we are hopeless, but we play because we enjoy it. The committee are only interested in teams that can win". Andy even had an article published in the Newcastle Evening Chronicle on 6th March 1982, pleading his case.

Barnstoneworth United were third from bottom of the under-18's league and second from bottom of the under-17's league.

"We are not quite bottom of the leagues because some teams don't turn up", said Andy. "When we were reported to the five-a-side committee we asked to be allowed to put our side of the argument and we were told to write a letter. I was told I would not be allowed to play football again until I apologised. I admit I might have used two or three words where one would have done, but I was not cheeky".

Andy wrote a letter to the committee suggesting "ways the administration of the club could be improved". After the ban the team decided to picket league meetings at the Station Road Club and collected 60 signatures on a petition form from fellow players.

(Rebel Andy Bowman is now a happily married father of three girls and is employed as a teacher at a school in Cornwall.)

Barnstoneworth United 1982 Andy Bowman, Angus Condie, David Humphrey and Scott Condie.

By 1984 Wallsend Boys' Club were able to start using some of their former stars to support themselves when needed. The presentation night of that year, held on July 19th, saw the launch of an appeal to raise £5000 for repairs to the roof, damaged in the fire of 1977 and never properly repaired, – in fact leaking in four places. Peter Beardsley, now a star of Newcastle United and England, having played for Vancouver Whitecaps since his signing for Carlisle, was happy to spearhead the appeal and lend his name to it. Professional players and former old Boys', Tony Sealy, Eric Steele, Les Taylor, Keith Lockhart and Brian Laws were the first to make donations, totalling £141. Neil McDonald, now also playing for Newcastle United lent his support as well. The club's boys committee handed over a cheque for £1,000 to Peter Beardsley from funds they had raised over a number of years. Launching the appeal Peter said that the Boys' Club movement was worth supporting. "I still remember the great pleasure I derived from being a member of, and playing for,

Support Peter's Appeal for the Boys' Club

Wallsend Boys' Club". By that time, Peter Beardsley was back on Tyneside and a star of the Newcastle United team. But his route there from WBC had not been a straightforward one.

Peter first arrived at Newcastle United in September of 1983 from Canada, where he had been playing football with Vancouver Whitecaps.

Rejection by Gillingham, Cambridge and Burnley as a teenager saw him embark on a career at

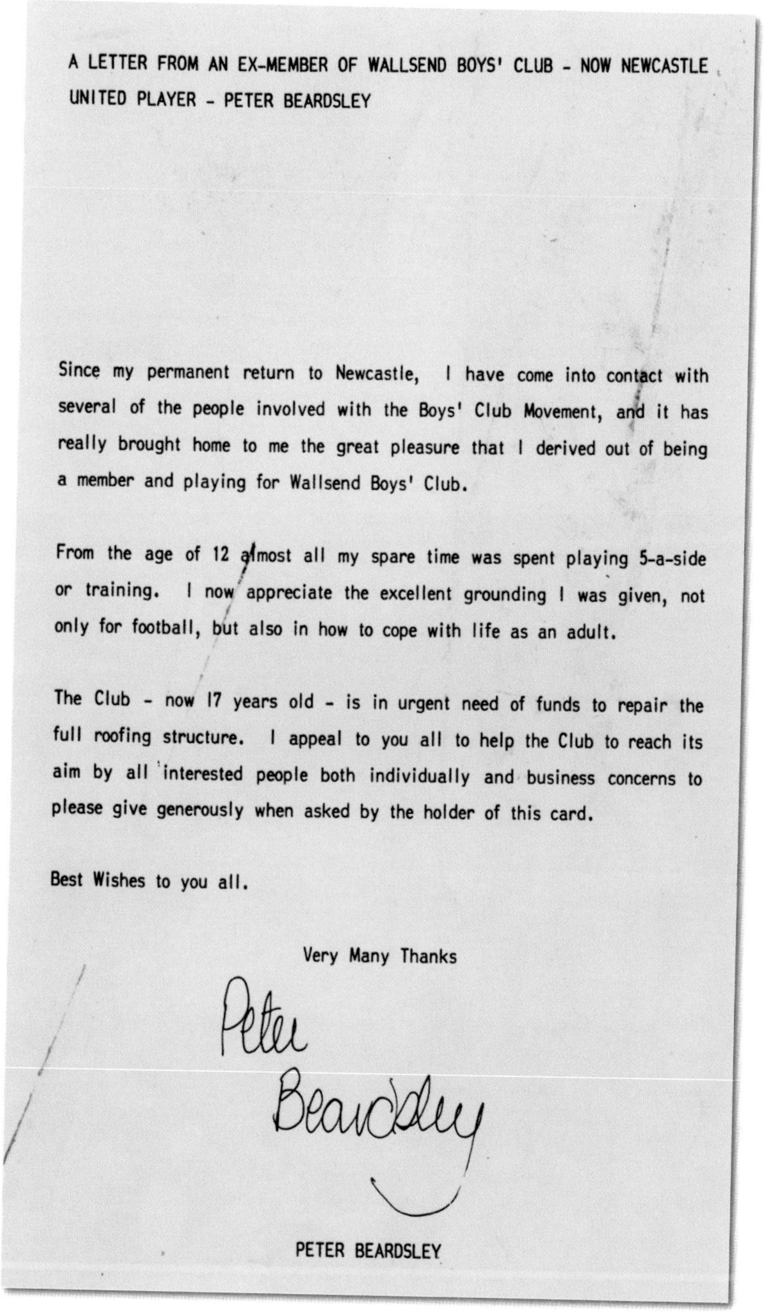

A LETTER FROM AN EX-MEMBER OF WALLSEND BOYS' CLUB - NOW NEWCASTLE UNITED PLAYER - PETER BEARDSLEY

Since my permanent return to Newcastle, I have come into contact with several of the people involved with the Boys' Club Movement, and it has really brought home to me the great pleasure that I derived out of being a member and playing for Wallsend Boys' Club.

From the age of 12 almost all my spare time was spent playing 5-a-side or training. I now appreciate the excellent grounding I was given, not only for football, but also in how to cope with life as an adult.

The Club - now 17 years old - is in urgent need of funds to repair the full roofing structure. I appeal to you all to help the Club to reach its aim by all interested people both individually and business concerns to please give generously when asked by the holder of this card.

Best Wishes to you all.

Very Many Thanks

Peter Beardsley

PETER BEARDSLEY

a local valve production factory on Tyneside. This was in spite of recommendations from Peter Kirkley.

"He was 11 when I first saw him", Peter Kirkley said. "He was the most skilful player I'd ever seen at that time."

Young Beardsley had apparently been obsessive about football. He slept with a football beside his bed and played four matches every weekend. His Puma Pele Rio boots were the love of his life. Yet the Beardsley on display to other teams when he went for trials was a small, shy boy. The Beardsley of Kirkley's experience was different. In his last match for Wallsend Boys' Club, a championship decider, Beardsley scored six in a 9-1 win, including one goal for which he won the ball on the halfway line, dazzled his way through the entire opposition team, fell on his hands and knees on the goal line and headed the ball into the net. Then Peter apologised to the goalkeeper. "I'm not taking the mickey, I've just always wanted to do that," he said.

Bobby Moncur, then at Carlisle, was the first manager to sign Beardsley. But then he was sold to the Vancouver Whitecaps.

As a 21 year old Beardsley was rejected by Ron Atkinson at Manchester United before Arthur Cox signed him at Newcastle for £150,000 in September 1983 to replace Imray Varadi and play alongside Kevin Keegan. In 1984 the Keegan-Beardsley-Waddle partnership was a great one for Newcastle and led to promotion into the old First Division in Keegan's goodbye season of 83/84.

Wallsend Boys' Club Football Team. With Steve Watson (left back row) and Robbie Elliott (second from left front row).

In that same year, the football conveyor belt of Wallsend Boys' club was continuing to roll.

They were to become, not just professional players, but Newcastle United players.

These were Steve Watson, Alan Thompson, Robbie Elliott and Lee Clark. All four also received England honours at under-21 or youth level.

At the same time at the club, though relatively unnoticed by scouts or the local press, was a fourteen year old player called Alan Shearer. It was not until Alan was 16, and had left WBC, that he got his first chance as a professional when Southampton signed him.

In the middle of all this excitement, Sid Sharp was eager to point out again in a newspaper interview that the club was "not just about producing stars. There are an awful lot of lads who don't make the grade but still have a good time.

Young lads Steve Watson, Alan Thompson, Robbie Elliott and Lee Clark.

They're now joiners, plumbers or civil servants but they come back to see us just like some of the professionals do and that's just as rewarding."

One such old boy, Les Howie, did make his mark on the football world, but not actually on the pitch.

In 1974, as a ten-year-old boy, Les joined Wallsend Boys' Club with the intention of playing five a side football. Thirty-two years later he had well and truly proven that, as an ex Wallsend Boys' Club member, you did not need to be a professional footballer, to make your mark in the sporting field in a big way. By the age of fifteen Les was refereeing five a side football leagues and was organising the under-10's and under-11's leagues at the club. In 1980 Les had started fun coaching for the younger players which was intended to give the players an appetite for the game and filter them into the five a side leagues, (Robert Slone taking on a similar coaching roll at a later date). The youngest 11-a-side league teams, in the early 1980s were under-13's, so Les started up under-11's and under-12's teams to play in coast colts competitions (only playing about four games a season). Les also started running the under-13's 11-a-side team, where they were runners up to North Shields in the Boys' Club league. Alan Shearer starting his first 11-a-side league

Young Les Howie.

football under Les in this league, after playing under-12's friendlies the previous season. Alan played 11-a-side football for Wallsend Boys' Club for five years and in the five-a-side league for one year. One of Alan's team mates in those early days was Brian Sweeney who now manages 11-a-side teams for Wallsend Boys' Club. Les was a volunteer leader at the Boys' Club from the age of fifteen until the age of twenty-five.

As well as his volunteer work at the Boys' Club Les became Trainee Recreation Officer at North Tyneside Council in 1982 at the age of eighteen, a post he held for two years. 1985 was the United Nations Year of Youth and to coincide with this, Les organised the first ever North Tyneside International Youth Football Tournament, which thanks to Les's foresight and imagination, is still flourishing today, with teams from as far away as Europe, Canada and the USA taking part. Les went to Sunderland University from 1986 to 1988, where he gained a degree in Youth Work.

He took on the job as full time leader at Blyth Town Boys' Club in September 1988, this position being held for eighteen months, before he came back to work for North Tyneside Council, as Young Peoples Services Manager.

A more mature Les Howie.

In 1990 Les was approached to become County Director of the Nottinghamshire Association of Boys' Clubs, a position he held until 1998. In 1992 he was a referee in the Paraplegic Olympics in Barcelona, which included taking charge of the semi-final between Holland and Ireland. He also ran football tournaments at Keele University, and coached the England Boys' Club's team for three seasons (1996-1998).

Les joined the Football Association in a full time roll in 1998 as Regional Director of Football Development moving on to the position of National Clubs Development Manager in 2000, where he brought Charter Status into youth football and helped to develop Mini Soccer. He also wrote the FA Level One Coaching Badge, which in its first three and a half years has produced over 100,000 qualified coaches.

In 2005 Les became the National Development Manager (Clubs and Coaches), for the FA. managing the nine regional coaches. Les has also written two football books published by "Hodder" the books' titles being "Football Parents" and "Running a Club", which he dedicated to Peter Kirkley and David Beardall.

With all this work involving extensive travelling, and being married with three young children. Les still finds time to do voluntary work and now holds the position of Chairman of the Nottinghamshire Association of Clubs for Young People, a position he has held since 1999.

Les has come a long, long way since turning up at Wallsend Boys' Club as a potential five-a-side player, at ten years of age in 1974, and is a marvellous example to others who have aspirations other than to become a professional footballer.

Although there was little competitive boxing in the club by the 1980s, there was still interest in the sport and in February 1984 the quarter-final bout of 'Henry Cooper's Golden Belt' took place in the club. This was a Boys' Club inter-city boxing tournament which was televised on Channel Four. In the quarter-final, South London fought Manchester and Newcastle fought Belfast. There seems to be no record of who actually won, but among the people who attended were Henry Cooper himself, Alan Minter and Maurice Hope. The event was clearly a success, because the following year the Final was held in the club and about 200 people turned up as spectators.

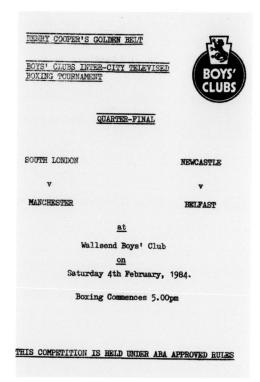

HENRY COOPER'S GOLDEN BELT

BOYS' CLUBS INTER-CITY TELEVISED
BOXING TOURNAMENT

BOYS' CLUBS

QUARTER-FINAL

SOUTH LONDON   NEWCASTLE

v   v

MANCHESTER   BELFAST

at

Wallsend Boys' Club

on

Saturday 4th February, 1984.

Boxing Commences 5.00pm

THIS COMPETITION IS HELD UNDER ABA APPROVED RULES

In 1985 another highlight was the visit to the club of the Duke of Gloucester, as President of the NABC, following in the footsteps of his father who had visited in 1956. The Duke met local dignitaries and club officials who showed him around the building. He was introduced to club members, who gave demonstrations of pool, table tennis, badminton and football.

The Duke was a smash hit with Council Chairman Jennie Shearan. He was playing table tennis when he hit a smash shot. The ball spun off the table towards Councillor Mrs Shearan, Chairman of Tyne Wear Council, and hit her, bringing apologies with a smile, watched also by the Lord Lieutenant of Tyne Wear, Sir Ralph Carr-Ellison. The Duke also tried pool, potting the first ball.

The Duke later visited six other Boys' clubs in Blyth, North Tyneside and Newcastle.

Glen Roeder, who played for Newcastle United, (and later managed Newcastle United) presented football trophies and awards to the members at the 1985 11-a-side presentation night for Wallsend Boys' Club.

In 1986 the press were hailing another footballing discovery from Wallsend Boys' Club, Lee Clark, who had modelled himself on his hero Peter Beardsley. Lee signed for Newcastle United at the age of 14 and played for them until 1997 before going to deadly rivals Sunderland, then Fulham, before returning to play for Newcastle in 2005 at the age of 32.

He is a classic example of the sort of professional players and coaches turned out by the Boys' Club.

In March 1986 Kader F. C. stayed at the Boys' Club for a long weekend.

On 10th July Paul Gascoigne visited the Boys' Club. October saw the visit of British Amateur Golf Champion David Curry, English Youth Champion, John Metcalf and Match Play Champion, James Eadington.

In 1987 Newcastle United snapped up another school centre forward Alan Thompson from Wallsend Boys' Club and offered a contract to his fellow Boys' Club member, Anthony Lormor. Alan a close friend of super boy Lee Clark had turned down offers from Spurs and Chelsea to stay at home with Newcastle United. He had also attracted the attention of Southampton, Everton, Manchester United and Nottingham Forest.

Newcastle United Youth Development Officer Peter Kirkley said, "It's been Alan's lifetime ambition to sign for his home town club".

Paul Gascoigne of Newcastle United. Shaking hands with Bill McNaughton, on a visit to Wallsend Boys' Club.

When he was nine years of age he was the first boy in the North East to gain a super skills award and when interviewed on TV he said he hoped to play for Newcastle United one day.

"At 11, Alan scored 112 out of 140 goals for High Farm Middle School in one season. Apart from being a close friend of Lee Clark, he was also the next-door neighbour of Anthony Lormor, who scored his first senior goal for United at Queen of the South in 1987. Alan also attended Newcastle United School of Excellence.

Alan Thompson when playing for Celtic.

Anthony Lormor was rewarded for some excellent performances as a teenage striker for Newcastle United. For Lormor who was at St. James's Park courtesy of the Youth Training Scheme had been offered a full time contract by manager Willie McFaul. "I like the way Anthony plays and I have seen enough of him to decide to give him his chance".

The local press later told Anthony's story in the following words:

"Lormor a strapping striker played the full 90 minutes against Monaco in a friendly and showed that he was not afraid to go in where it hurts and his attitude was first class. But the then 17 year old from Ashington was very much a goal scorer. Lormor, a product of Wallsend Boys' Club, attracted Newcastle's attention when he helped himself to an incredible 80 goals for Wallsend Boys' Club in 1985. Lormor made his first team debut for Newcastle while he was still on the Y.T.S. replacing Mirandinha against Spurs at St. James's Park in January of 1988."

Anthony Lormor.

"On his first two full appearances for Newcastle United he scored each time and looked to have a terrific future. Yet he was hardly given another opportunity at Newcastle and left to join Lincoln in 1990 having played in eight games for United scoring three times. Lormor was City's leading scorer in his first three seasons and later scored in Chesterfield's play-off final at Wembley in 1994-95 season. Anthony played for Hartlepool, when injury struck again and he decided to combine being a referee with playing - something of a unique situation. Crippled by a succession of injuries throughout his career, the former Newcastle United striker had quit at the age of 32. Lormor had officially ended his career with Conference club Telford. He had taken a position as a full-time salesman but would continue in football as a referee - he'd already run the line at Gateshead's International Stadium while playing for Hartlepool."

In May 1988 the BBC screened the first documentary about the Football side of the club, focussing especially on Peter Beardsley and other leading players. The programme was called "Black and White…And Red All Over". The club were paid the princely sum of £30 for their assistance in making the programme.

The small sum paid for this programme paled into significance against the running cost being incurred. By 1989, once again the club were in need of major financial support, this time to raise £19000 for a suspended ceiling. Ex member Brian Laws, by then a player for Nottingham Forest, led on this appeal.

"Since I left Wallsend to move into the professional game I have never forgotten my roots, especially Wallsend Boys' Club, where football scouts first noticed me. The Boys' Club put me on the right road to the top and I have a lot to thank them for. I was only too pleased to help them appeal for a new suspended ceiling for the club".

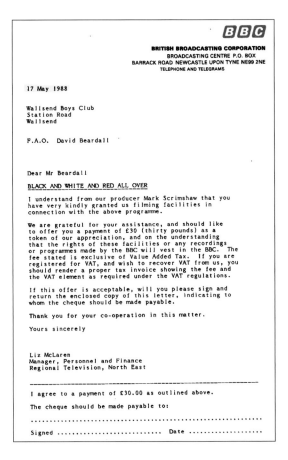

The football presentation night the same year saw players from Newcastle United, Paul Cannell, David Robinson and David Roche present trophies to the members.

The New Years Eve Patrons Party was held at Wallsend Boys' Club on Sunday 31st December, 7pm until midnight. As in previous years Patrons were offered a table of their own for the night with floor service both for drinks and buffet. Over the years the numbers attending the party had grown with the number of tickets now restricted to 180. People were making reservations for tickets months before the event.

The buffet was plated and served to the table. The Boys' Committee asked for the prize raffle to be drawn on the night. Donated prizes for the raffle were greatly appreciated. Wallsend Boys' Club, celebrated its 25th Anniversary in July 1990, (having opened for business in their current building in 1965) and a galaxy of stars attended the Lindisfarne Social Club on West Street, Wallsend, to mark their achievements. Such had been the footballing success of the "new" Wallsend Boys' Club since it was re-opened that Peter Kirkley, as both Newcastle United Youth Development Officer and the man who had started off the 11-a-side football teams at the club, was asked to produce a list of the Boys' Club players who made it into the Football League.

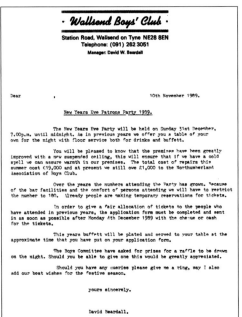

He did better than that; he came up with three teams of ex Wallsend Boys' Club youngsters who had made their mark in the League. His selections were:

First XI
Eric Steele (Derby County), Brian Laws (Nottingham Forest), Steve Bruce (Manchester United), Rob Hindmarch (Derby County), Neil McDonald (Everton), Les Taylor (Watford), Ian Bogie (Preston), Paul Stephenson (Millwall), Peter Beardsley (Liverpool), Ray Hankin (Leeds United), Lee Clark (Newcastle United).

Second XI
David Lawson (Everton), Steve Baker (Southampton), Jeff Wrightson (Preston), Chris Hedworth (Barnsley), Paul Baker (Hartlepool), Gary Leonard (West Brom), Tony Sealey (QPR), Mick Tait (Portsmouth), Alan Shearer (Southampton), Alan Waddle (Liverpool), Anth Lormor (Lincoln).

The third XI is not in the normal formation but is:
Paul Malcolm (Doncaster), Ian McKenzie (Stockport), David Roche (Newcastle), Keith Lockhart (Wolves), Gordon Nesbit (West Brom), Derrick Parker (Burnley), Phil Ray (Burnley), Phil Cavener (Burnley), Kevin Smith (Cambridge), Barry Wardrobe (Sunderland), David Robinson (Newcastle). Peter said in his speech, "That is a fabulous record by any standards, and I've only included players who have made the grade. You could add another 30 players who have gone on to Football League clubs without hitting the headlines".

Within a few weeks of that list being drawn up it was virtually redundant with new players emerging from the Boys' Club. In December 1990 Steve Watson became the youngest ever player for Newcastle United when he stepped on as substitute at Wolverhampton, at the age of 16 years and 223 days. Steve was the fourth 16-year old to play for Newcastle after Paul Ferris, Jock Finlay and Neil McDonald, but at 16 years 223 days, he was the youngest by 72 days. Ironically he had followed the path of McDonald, who started at Wallsend Boys' Club before moving on to Newcastle and Everton.

Steve hoped to be just as successful."I don't model myself on anybody, but I'd love to be as good as players like Peter Beardsley and Neil McDonald who both started their careers at the Boys' Club. It was a thrill coming on at Molineux - the best moment of my life. Now I'm more determined than ever to make it to the top. All the players have made me feel welcome and Lee Clark has been particularly helpful"

Just as all the celebrations of past and present success were underway; another problem hit the club with yet another fire breaking out on June 17th 1990. The Fire Report read as follows:

Time of call:	1855 Hrs
Address of fire:	Wallsend Boys' Club, Station Road
Name of Occupier:	Mrs Dodds
Where fire started.	Sports Hall, ground floor
Cause of fire:	Overheating of faulty electrical circuit
Damage to item first ignited:	Quantity of PVC Electrical Insulation destroyed by fire
Damage to room of origin:	Explorer video game machine slightly damaged by fire, smoke and fire brigade personnel
	5% of Sports Hall slightly damaged by smoke.

The Borough Council will forward an invoice for £21 + VAT in due course to you because 2 Major pumps, Northumbria Police and NEEB attended.

Cause: The supposed cause of the fire is a matter of opinion and not fact and is based on a brief and necessary examination of the evidence available. If a more detailed and specialised investigation is carried out, and there is no requirement for the Fire Brigade to do so, facts may well be discovered which will alter the present opinion.

Acting Station Officer Mr K. Jackson

Fortunately on this occasion damage seems to have been fairly limited, mainly smoke damage to the Sports Hall. It was soon put right, and by the following late summer bank holiday the club premises were used for possibly their most unusual event so far – an exhibition of Herpetology, otherwise known as snakes and lizards. Among the stars of this particular show was a giant Indian Python called Rishma.

Within days of this successful and popular exhibition, Wallsend Boys' Club was in the news again, as angry residents reacted to the shocking news that the club was being faced with such financial struggles that it might well have to close. This particular crisis had been brought on by a cut in the grant given by the local council, from £18000 to just £10000. One good thing about the crisis was that it demonstrated clearly how valued the club was by many people in Wallsend. They pointed out that it had over 1000 members, boys and girls now, and that it provided a drop-in centre for unemployed young people as well as an after school key club for children of working parents. The press coverage included the following:

Gripping attraction

■ The eyes have it as Kim Brown has a decko at her Leopard gecko at the show in Wallsend Boys' Club.

TIPPING the scales at a Bank Holiday exhibition in Wallsend were the stars of the show — reptiles and amphibians.

Intrepid visitors to this year's show organised by the Northern Herpetological Society were able, if brave enough, to come to grips with a special attraction — a giant Indian Python named Rishma.

The organisers said the show was one of the most comprehensive collections of scaley creatures ever held in the region, giving show-goers the chance to see animals never before dislayed by the society.

John Hackworth, the society's se-

By SEAN HARAN

cretary, said: "Herpetology is one of the fastest growing hobbies in Britain. And a number of Britain's top breeders attended the show bringing a large number of captive-bred species with them."

The show at Wallsend Boy's Club, Station Road, aimed to give newcomers to the hobby advice on breeding and keeping reptiles.

And the snakes and lizards will be waiting for more enthusiasts coming to see them today between 10am and 5pm.

Leader David Beardall said "All members have been contacted for their help in keeping the club going." "The council has helped us in the past. They have always provided us with a grant, and two years ago gave us financial assistance to carry out work on the ceiling, but the club costs so much a year to run. We are open seven days a week and provide a real service to many people. We can only ask members to pay so much or they will not be able to afford to come".

One mother, Mrs Margaret Richardson of Hadrian Park, Wallsend, said "The council must realise there is little enough for young people in Wallsend to do without closing this vital social and sporting meeting place". She claimed that without the club, the vandalism rate was bound to rise, leaving the council to pick up the bill.

Wallsend News Guardia

Thursday, August 29, 1991

VFD certified dl:
to December,

'Club provides a lot for the young people down here'

Finance crisis poses threat to boys' club

Said Mr Beardall "Unless we get the extra money we will have to close which will be a great shame. The club provides a lot for the young people down here. It was where Peter Beardsley learned to play football, but it isn't just the football, it's a community club".

A spokesman for North Tyneside Council said that the situation was being reviewed. This was being looked at in the same way that they would look at any appeal of this nature."

Once again the club survived. The campaign clearly bore fruit and the original grant was reinstated.

Still the football story went on. An article in the press in 1990 had Jim Smith, Newcastle United manager, praising the contribution that young players like Lee Clark, Steve Watson, David Roche, David Robinson, and Tommy Heron were making to his team.

"They have all come in at one time or another and played like men. I'm really heartened. The kids have been great. In terms of attitude and ability you just can't fault them. Their talent is a huge bonus, not just for today but for the future as well. You are lucky at a football club if two or three youngsters make the grade, here there are six or seven pushing through and that's a hell of a percentage. They won't all make it, but we have a tremendous amount of talent on tap".

Another story at the time was a reminder of the precarious nature of the footballer's career with Alan Thompson facing a struggle to survive in the game. On 14th December he was set to undergo a crucial operation in a bid to save his career.

Alan, who fractured his neck in a five-player car crash, had been wearing a neck brace since September. The specialist had recommended an operation in the hope that the 16-year-old youngster would play again. Alan was in line for a place in the England Under-17 side before the horror car crash.

Now he was fighting for his future. Even at the best he faced a year out of the game. Alan admitted that if he did not have the operation he wouldn't play again; it was as simple as that. If he had the operation he would take the chance and hope for the best. There was a risk involved in the operation, but physiotherapist Derek Wright said, "If everything is solid, Alan will have a real chance of playing again". Thankfully, the operation was successful.

Kenny Pattinson was a member of Wallsend Boys' Club from 1980 to 1990. He excelled in the 5-a-side leagues, playing for many teams, including "Hibs", "Ardeeonions" and "Lancers". Despite his lack of inches he was always a handful for any team. Kenny then became a jockey with one of the top stables at Newmarket.

Kenny Pattinson (right hand side front row) with his five a side team.

Kenny riding "Fatack". The 2nd horse.

Kenny never fails to visit the Club when he is in the area. He is another example of how it is not just pro footballers who come out of the Boys' Club.

By late January 1991 during F A Cup week old boys from WBC were playing in 6 of the cup ties.

The Club members could be forgiven for having divided loyalties. First they would be concerned to learn whether Peter Beardsley was fit to play for Liverpool against Brighton. But they would also want to know whether Steve Bruce and Manchester United were successful in their defence of the Cup against Bolton, and how Millwall's Paul Stephenson would play against Sheffield Wednesday.

Southampton's strike force at Coventry would include Alan Shearer, who scored twice while facing Bruce in the Rumbelows Cup at Old Trafford on the Wednesday, while on the Sunday, Everton's Neil McDonald, who had already confronted Beardsley in an all-Mersey Wembley final, would step out against non-league Woking.

The Monday's second replay between Nottingham Forest and Crystal Palace would decide whether Brian Laws' club Forest would visit Newcastle. And Newcastle's youngest ever first team player, Steve Watson, was involved in that. Lee Clark would be a Newcastle substitute.

Old Trafford vice captain Steve Bruce summed up the "stars" affection for their old club in Station Road, Wallsend as. "A marvellous place, probably unique.

I was a member there for five years. I'd be there four or five nights a week. Peter Beardsley,

Rob Hindmarch and I were in the same team. It was great to be part of the club."

In the October Gavin Fell took part in the Radio 5 show "Ring a Winner" which was broadcast on a Sunday starting 12.05pm and ending at 1.40pm along with ex Boys' Club member Brian Laws.

Gavin had been a member of the Boys' Club for five years and had signed schoolboy forms for Wimbledon. The Sunday broadcast brought some valuable publicity for the Boys' Club.

The Management Committee of Wallsend Boys' Club held their usual Patrons' New Years Eve Party on Tuesday 31st December.

They had a new double act "His N Hers" who provided a wide selection of records for dancing from

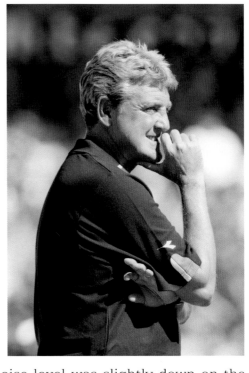

the fifties through to the hit records of the day. The noise level was slightly down on the previous year, to keep neighbouring homes happy. The meal was, as in previous years served at the table. It included Two Cold Meats, Chicken Drum Stick, Prawns, Gala Pie, Ocean Stick, Smoked Mackerel and the salads. The Bar facilities included draught McEwans Larger, McEwans Best Scotch and Federation Special. Most types of spirits and soft drinks were also available.

Patrons were able to reserve their tables in advance and waiter service was used to serve drinks to the tables. Special lighting effects were arranged as in previous years. The cost of the ticket was £8, which did not include any transport, Senior Boys' Club Members acted as waiters on the night and hoped for some generous tips from happy customers.

The New Year of 1992 began with yet another party, this one a belated 25th anniversary of the opening of the club building. On January 7th a cocktail party was held with guests including many who had helped the club over the previous quarter century. The Lord Lieutenant, Sir Ralph Carr-Ellison, was again in attendance and officially opened a refurbished canteen. "This I feel was a splendid occasion with a good cross section of persons who have helped the club over the 25 years, since the club re-opened."

According to press coverage Sir Ralph apologised for not being able to meet everyone during the evening, but said he did enjoy his visit to the club and wished the management, staff and members every success in the future years.

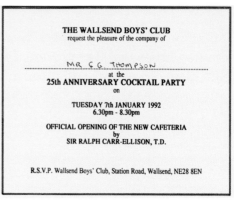

THE WALLSEND BOYS' CLUB
request the pleasure of the company of

MR C G THOMPSON
at the
25th ANNIVERSARY COCKTAIL PARTY
on

TUESDAY 7th JANUARY 1992
6.30pm - 8.30pm

OFFICIAL OPENING OF THE NEW CAFETERIA
by
SIR RALPH CARR-ELLISON, T.D.

R.S.V.P. Wallsend Boys' Club, Station Road, Wallsend, NE28 8EN

Dave Beardall was quoted as saying, "One must give a big vote of thanks to our Treasurer who was able to find a sponsor who supplied the wines and the finger buffet for the occasion at no cost to the club, also everyone who helped to set up the photograph display, flowers, bar and general help without which it would not have been possible to have such a super occasion. I hope that everyone who attended the evening enjoyed himself or herself and that we could have another celebration when the club will be 50 years old in 1988, since the foundation of the club was in 1938".

Inevitably many of the write-ups in the local press referred to the roll call of professional players produced over the previous 25 years, but there was also a mention of ex-member Gordon Sumner, who had of course gone on to become the international rock star Sting. As Gordon Sumner he had played regular five-a-side football at the Boys' Club. He still remembered the Boys' Club with affection and in the recent past purchased a number of their 'Wallsend to Wembley' tee shirts.

Meanwhile the regular work of the club continued with volunteers giving of their time in club committee meetings like this one, from the Boys' Committee, recorded from 1992.

1992. Part of the minutes of the Boys' Committee meeting.

Present: Ian Ruddick, Anthony Hampton, Steven Darmody, Michael Gill, Michael Carrick, Chris Hood and Kevin Urwin.

Also present was Peter Mays, Chairman of the Boys' Club, who chaired the meeting.
        Election of Chairman ....Ian Ruddick.
        Election of Secretary...................Anthony Hampton.
        Election of Treasurer ....Steven Darmody.

Working Rota.

The under mentioned volunteered to work on the following days.
        Ian Ruddick................................Mondays and Sundays.
        Anthony Hampton ....Mondays, Tuesdays and Thursdays.
        Steven Darmody ....Tuesdays and Wednesdays.
        Michael Gill................................Tuesdays, Wednesdays and Thursdays.
        Michael Carrick..........................Saturdays and Sundays.
        Chris Hood.................................Tuesdays, Fridays and Sundays.
        Kevin Urwin...............................Saturdays and Sundays.

The Boys' Committee felt that to accommodate other sports, the five-a-side pitch should be marked out for different sports eg, Basketball, Badminton etc.

One of the boys giving of their time in this way, 11 year old Michael Carrick, was soon to be recognised as the latest big footballing star to emerge from the club.

In April 1992 the club tried, not for the first time, to address the issue of allowing girls regular access to the club. They gave one night a week over to the girls, but it was not deemed a success in the end, and the council felt that premises and amenities were not suitable for the girls. After five months the experiment was stopped for the time being.

March 20th 1993 saw another big amateur boxing event held in the club, although they had to borrow their boxing ring from Blyth Town Boys' Club. This was the North East Boxing Championship Regional Finals.

The Boys' club laid on a full canteen service for boxers and visitors and this was the clubs first chance to really show off the refurbished canteen, which worked extremely well on the day.
For any one wishing to partake in alcoholic beverages, they were directed to the local Comrades Club.

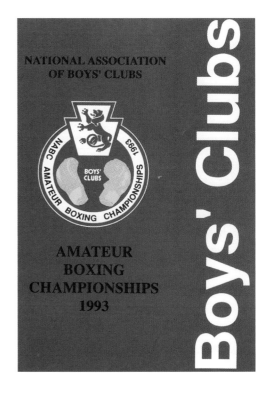

The NABC Boxing Championships were one of the major youth boxing events held in Great Britain, involving some 1,000 young men between the ages of 15-19 in three class categories.

Class A – 15 years; Class B – 16 years; Class C – 17-19 years.

These culminated in three finals held in prestigious venues.

Class A at the Marriott Hotel, Bristol; Class B at the Mayfair Suite, Newcastle; and Class C at the Royal Lancaster Hotel, London.

A one-week Boxing Scholarship was awarded to winners of each weight under the guidance of the A.B.A. National Coaching Team. Blyth Town Boys' Club loaned the club their boxing ring, which was erected by Wallsend Boys' Club officials.

The Club Leader's Report for1992/ 1993 read as follows:
"I start my report this year, as with last year, to record a cut in the level of **Grant Aid** we receive from North Tyneside Council. This has meant that no part-time staff has been employed during this financial year. The figures opposite show the amounts of Grant Aid given over the last seven years and the projected figure for this financial year.

1986/87 ....£16,390
1987/88 ....£17,058
1988/89 ....£18,817
1989/90 ....£19,671
1990/91 ....£19,443
1991/92 ....£18,000
1992/93 ....£17,207
1993/94 ....£16,000

Girls Session
Under the guide lines of the Council the club from 1st April 1992 gave one night over to a girl's session. This session was offered free and no payment for entrance or donation was given. By the end of August the staff that were employed by the Council felt that the premises were not a suitable environment for this session.
This cost the club a considerable amount of income over five months.

Repairs and Renovations
During the summer months we carried out repairs to the fencing around our perimeter grounds, painting of the clubs interior and new storage cupboards were built upstairs. A Government Scheme based at North Shields carried out all these projects.

Equipment
The club purchased a Silex Machine for the canteen, which can cook bacon, eggs and beef burgers etc, also a portable hot plate that can keep all meals hot for visiting parties or large catering functions.

We also obtained at very little cost, a floor polishing machine, a wet suction vacuum machine, chairs, a commercial toaster and other various pieces of equipment for the canteen from the Newcastle Health Authority. We are indebted to a patron of our club, Mr Colin Osborne, for obtaining this vital equipment, which saved the club a considerable amount of money.

Visiting Groups
During the year the club has hosted several groups who have stayed in our premises. (Breakfast and evening meal) They bring their own sleeping bags, sleep on the judo mats and have the use of the premises and play football matches against our own eleven-a-side teams and maybe a visit to St. James's Park. This brings a good income into the club funds.

Activities
The club continues with its main activity of football and our five-a-side section has leagues from under-17 down to under-9. The presentations took place last July and Lee Clark from Newcastle United did the honours.

Lee, was now the North East Footballer of the Year and as a former member of the club we offered him our congratulations and to Newcastle United on their excellent season. However, it does effect our "Gate money" when they have an evening match.

Our eleven-a-side teams have had another successful season with over twenty trophies being won. They took three teams to the N.A.B.C. International Tournament and won two age groups and were runners-up in the third, a feat never achieved before by any Boys' club. Our congratulations to all the players, and also a big thank you to Sid Sharp and his Army of Team Managers and helpers, who have brought all the success to Wallsend.

The club has four separate Martial Arts Groups, Judo, Kick Boxing, Karate and Wing Ching. We also have ladies Keep Fit Class on Monday afternoons.

Members have taken part in the N.A.B.C. Athletics, Cross Country and Quiz Competitions and won trophies in all of these events.

Finance

In order to increase our income, as a result of the cuts in the Grant Aid the Committee were forced to increase the members subscriptions in October 1992 from 30p to 40p and also an increase was made on the Hall hire of £1 to make the Hall hire now £13 per hour. This should produce an extra £2,000 over this financial year.

Staffing

The lack of paid staff has been a major problem, and my role as a full time worker would have been impossible without the help of a band of volunteers. To all these persons, too many to mention, thanks for a job well done.

David Beardall (Club Leader);

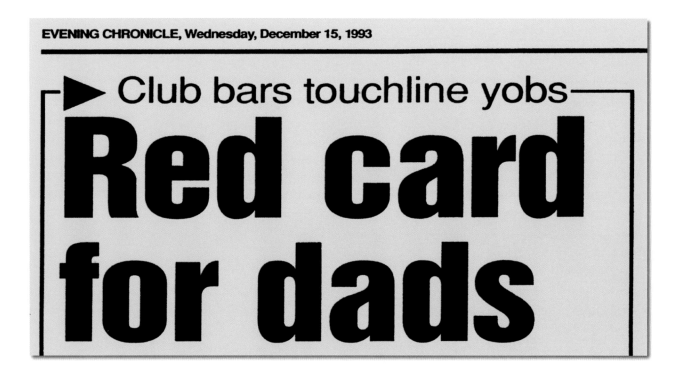

EVENING CHRONICLE, Wednesday, December 15, 1993

► Club bars touchline yobs

Red card for dads

In December 1993 reference was made in local newspapers to problems with parents causing problems on the touchline at both eleven-a-side and five-a-side football matches. Football mad dads who wanted to see their sons become superstars were turning into touchline yobs. Threats and foul language turned the air blue when parents arrived to cheer on their youngsters.

A court was told how rivalry between under-11-sides from South Shields and Sunderland spilled over into violence at a presentation evening. Sunderland magistrates fined one father for assault and obstructing police after adults joined in the mayhem.

David Beardall was quoted as saying that dads can make it tough for the youngsters from the touchlines. "This club has produced players of the calibre of Newcastle's Peter Beardsley, Lee Clark and Robbie Elliott.

But I have banned two parents after their shouting at players upset staff and youngsters during a five-a-side game. We can get as many as 200 adults to watch a game here; it's like a small St. James's Park.

Parents can get too carried away, too involved sometimes. Maybe it's the fathers trying to play the game through their sons. Boys as young as nine have been reduced to tears because of instructions shouted at them by anxious parents.

The parents should leave the coaching of the team to the managers."

In 1994 Wallsend Boys' Club were asked to take part in the Wallsend Festival procession around the Town. A lorry was acquired, and boy's club members, parents and Committee were dressed in various football strips, old and new.

Players on the float from left to right. Garry Collingwood, Chris Thorman (who went on to play for Huddersfield Rugby League Team), Michael Gill, Chris Hood, Michael Carrick and Craig Heward.

Parents and Committee taking part are from left to right, Brian Collingwood, Bill McNaughton, Jim O' Brien, Kevin Whately (Actor), Peter Mays and Brian Hall.

By the mid 1990s finance was again becoming a pressing issue.

In 1994 Swan Hunter's closed its doors. The old firm was no more. This was a devastating blow for the whole town, and indeed much of Tyneside, but it was also the end of an era for the club.

Swan's had been faithful supporters of the club for over 50 years. Clearly other sponsorship would be needed, and indeed did eventually come.

But it could definitely be said to be the end of an era for Wallsend Boys' Club with the severing of the 'Swan Connection'.

Chapter 11 - Into the 21st Century: a new era 1994-2003

In June 1994 Wallsend Boys' Club was privileged to have a visit from Clive Tyldsley of the B.B.C. T V. programme, "Sportsnight". He was there to make a documentary drawing out the links between Swan's and what had become known as the football nursery of Wallsend Boys' Club.

In July Robbie Elliott and Steve Watson of Newcastle United came along and presented trophies and medals to the members at the annual 11-a-side presentation night.

In the same month Wallsend Boys' Club under-13's were playing in the "Dana Cup" under the name of North Tyneside, this was because North Tyneside Council was twinned with "Frederikshavn Kommune". The team were invited to Frederikshavn partly to play football, partly to advertise North Tyneside and partly to get inspiration to hold a tournament of the same style as the "Dana Cup". Two of North Tyneside Council's representatives made the journey to Denmark with the Boys' Club.

"It's fantastic to be here; all the houses look new and it's so clean", said Steve Howie, one half of the North Tyneside's coaching duo. The other half Ken Richardson admitted that he was envious of the facilities that Frederikshavn could offer their residents.

Robbie Elliott presenting a prize
to Stephen Hutchinson.

Wallsend under-13's had six of their squad that trained once a week with professional clubs, either at Sunderland, Newcastle, Middlesbrough or Manchester United. Michael Frederiksen, from Frederikshavn, said, "North Tyneside's playing style is not typical British, the Green and yellow shirted Englishmen try all the time to play "Position play". It is in fact a pleasure to watch them play."

When the team had played its last game, the players and representatives spent a day at Farup Sommerland, where free entrance for "Dana Cup" participants was given.

North Tyneside Council thanked "Twin Town" Frederikshavn for the hospitality shown to everyone on the trip. They had a great time.

In 1994 an article in "Night and Day" showed the national interest that there was in the phenomenal success of Wallsend Boys' Club as producers of great footballers. In interviews with Peter Kirkley and Sid Sharp it tried to sum up the success the club had had in the past, but also highlighted the promising future of the latest star, 13 year old Michael Carrick.

"Portrait of a Boys' Club" focussed on the comments of Peter Kirkely and Sid Sharp and gave a great insight into the work of 'talent spotting' that had gone on for years in Wallsend Boys' Club and others like it. It pointed out that for 25 years Sid and his predecessors had unearthed a rich seam of footballing talent from the area. Sid also paid tribute in the article to the work of Peter Kirkley.

"Kirkley, according to Sid Sharp, has the finest eye for a young footballer in the country. "You cannot value the number of players he has spotted over the years", he says.

He is a remarkable man, and quite rightly he is now the second best - known man in football on Tyneside - after Kevin Keegan. You've got to count him ahead of most of the stars of the team - because he discovered them!"

"The conveyor belt goes on", says Sid in the article. "I saw a boy called Michael Carrick playing in a school game a few years ago. The double brandy hit me straight away! He had a fantastic sense of balance, he could think and move quickly, and he always had his head up looking around, reading the game. He was a natural".

Michael was then 13 and had the following clubs interested in him; Arsenal, Crystal Palace, Chelsea, West Ham, Wimbledon, Swindon, Nottingham Forest, Middlesbrough, Newcastle and Everton. "Enough to turn a boys head, you would think," said the journalist. "Not so, in the half hour I spent with Michael talking about his hopes and dreams, he was if anything, rather downbeat about his chances, constantly replying, "There's a long way to go yet" to every bid to get him to amplify on his future. Both he, and his brother Graeme, nine, who shows signs of being every bit as good as his brother, and attends the Newcastle United School of Excellence, seemed the not in the least bit big headed about their achievements."

The confident predictions about Michael's future bore fruit in 1998 when he was signed up by West Ham for whom he played until 2004 before transferring to Tottenham Hotspur.

Peter Kirkley.

Sid Sharp.

In November 1994 there was a special event for a very special person connected with the Boys' Club. This event was a timely reminder that, no matter how important football was in Wallsend Boys' Club, the club's values were always focused on more fundamental things as well. The occasion in question took place in the Cathedral of football, St. James's Park to celebrate the achievement of one of the unsung heroes of the club.

David Gilray took the salute of 26,000 fans at St. James's Park before the England under-21 football match against Ireland. England under-21 full back Steve Watson presented David with an F.A. award for the outstanding work he had done for Wallsend Boys' Club.

The previous month David was given the prestigious Keystone Award from the National Association of Boys' Clubs, for services rendered.

Newcastle United manager Kevin Keegan was also on hand to congratulate David who had been a member at Wallsend Boys' Club for 22 years.

David had overcome severe physical disabilities to play an active role in the clubs activities. Club Secretary Bill McNaughton said, "David sums up the spirit of what Boys' Clubs are all about. When he joined the Boys' Club David had difficulty walking and friends had to bring him and collect him in the car. Later David ran a five-a-side team and even played in goal in friendly matches now and again."

As the lack of support from Swan's began to take effect, the club again found itself in financial crisis.

Once again famous old boys were called upon to support new sponsorship deals. Peter Beardsley, now captain of Newcastle United turned out in November 1995 to endorse a sponsorship deal from Northumbrian Water which meant a cash donation, strips for the under -13 side and sweatshirts for another 120 players. The United skipper turned up to seal the deal with under-13 skipper Marc Jarvis, and his dad Alan Jarvis who was a coach at the club. The night before Peter had lined up at St. James's Park against another graduate of the Wallsend Boys' Club production line, Blackburn's Geordie striker Alan Shearer.

Such sponsorship, though vital and much appreciated, was not really enough to keep the club secure however.

As financial pressure grew in the mid 1990s there were fears that the club would actually fold under the pressure. Sid Sharp, again interviewed by the media in 1996, put the problem out into the open.

He said, "There is nowhere in this country with this club's record of producing professional footballers. In 30 years we have provided the game with millions of pounds of talent, yet the clubs have not put a single penny back, and it is crippling for us. …We need £7000 a year just to survive and we have to raise every last penny ourselves."

This financial problem was particularly ironic at a time when, on 30th July 1996, Newcastle United paid out a record £15 million for their latest transfer, ex-Wallsend Boys' Club player, Alan Shearer. What an incredible thought – an ex-Wallsend Boys' Club player was now the world's most expensive footballer!

Alan had been born in Gosforth and attended Gosforth High School, but began his footballing days with Wallsend Boys' Club. He had always maintained his career would not be complete without playing for Newcastle United. He had a trial with Newcastle in 1986 when he was just 16. Sadly for them, they stuck him in goal and didn't sign him. In 1987 he travelled to the south coast to join Southampton as a YTS trainee and his career really got started. In April 1988, Alan became the youngest player to score a hat trick on his first division debut, a record previously held by the legendary Jimmy Greaves.

The man who discovered Alan, the then 75 year old football scout Jack Hixon, was quoted in the press at the time as saying that it was fabulous his protégé was finally coming home. Jack had spotted Alan's raw talent watching him play for Newcastle Boys and supervised his move to Southampton. The player and his mentor remained close friends from then on. In February 1992 Alan had made his England debut and in July 1992 he was transferred for £3.5m, to Blackburn. Four years on, his value had more than quadrupled.

By the time Alan Shearer retired from playing in the summer of 2006, just as this History was being written, his reputation had grown beyond all imaginings back in 1986 when he had that first trial for Newcastle. He had not only captained his beloved Newcastle and England, he held the record for most goals scored by any single player in the Premiership, and had broken Jackie Milburn's record to become Newcastle United's most prolific ever goal scorer. Also in keeping with the reputation he had also developed as a very decent individual, Alan's farewell testimonial match at St James' Park in May 2006 raised £1.6 million for various charities, including a donation of £15000 to Wallsend Boys' Club.

But back in 1996 the club who had helped give him his first taste of competitive football were struggling for survival financially.

Two letters were published in the local press in August 1996 in response to a plea by Wallsend Boys' Club about their lack of finances and their struggle to make ends meet.

SPORT 14   DAILY EXPRESS, MONDAY AUGUST 12, 1996

THE BIG KICK-OFF

Club that found Shearer is struggling to survive

"I was saddened this week, as I'm sure were many others, to hear of the plight of Wallsend Boys' Club. The great breeding ground for professional footballers is without any secure funding and its future is under threat.

Although not widely publicised, the club has in the past been backed by the tremendous contribution made by Swan Hunters, but its closure has affected a great loss. Consequently, financial support is desperately needed. In recent years the talent of some of our great players has been developed through the club. Coincidentally, it has only recently been reported in the media (and acknowledged by certain professionals) there is too much money floating around in the game and player's wages are too high. Ironic, isn't it!

If each of the players who came up through the ranks of Wallsend dipped into their "surplus" funds and contributed the equivalent of one week's wages, this would provide sufficient security through to the next century.
After all, what is in effect a minor personal contribution would give this great club hope for prosperity.

Without this, the opportunity these individuals were given to develop their skills will be snatched from the youth of today, which will undoubtedly be detrimental to the future success of the game we love.

So come on lads, put your hands in your pockets, tip out your "loose change" and return the compliment. Many a player owes Wallsend Boys' Club more than just a thank you.

From Derek Brydon, Kingston Park."

Don't let this great club die

"I was shocked and disgusted to receive a letter from Wallsend Boys' Club, **explaining that North Tyneside Council intended to reduce its grant** to them by £10,000 this year. This cash cut will most certainly result in the clubs closure. The clubs letter asks everyone to write to his or her local councillor, urging them to support the Boys' Club and help in keeping this established building open. I want to make this situation public and draw to the attention of all parents and children, past, present and future, for the need to encourage the local council to keep the Boys' Club useable.

I have two boys who use it regularly, my husband, who as a youngster played football for the club, is now involved very heavily in coaching an 11-a-side team, and coaching the children in the skills of football.

He, like countless others, assists in the running of 11-a-side and 5-a-side league teams, and does it purely and simply because they want to, they do not expect or look for any financial gain. They give up their free time just to keep children happy and busy.

Girls too attend and participate in the various activities available, and the club is not just used for football purposes, there are a range of other sports and community uses.

Surely, North Tyneside Council realises there is little enough for the youth of Wallsend to do without closing this vital social and sporting meeting place. Surely they must see the need to keep it open. At the end of the day closure will most certainly put a bigger strain on the finances and resources of local government.

They must see that closure will only cause problems in the long term.
I feel sure that without this Boys' Club keeping children busy and off the street, the vandalism rate will certainly rise, leaving the council to pick up the bill. If the local council cannot be persuaded to reverse their decision, and this certainly looks most unlikely, the Boys' Club may have to close at the end of September.

Please help us to try and stop this from happening. From Mrs Margaret Richardson, Hadrian Park "

Boys' club saved from closure

Perhaps as a result of public concern, September saw a reprieve for the club, as reported in the local press.

"Wallsend Boys' Club were facing severe financial problems after North Tyneside Council slashed thousands of pounds in grant aid as part of its budget savings. However, there has been a change of heart from the council, as local councillors were inundated with protest letters from club members and local residents. The protest was so great that the council then decided to reinstate the full £18,000 grant aid. Club leader David Beardall said, "The grant was originally to be cut from £18,000 to £10,000 which would have left us in an impossible position. We wrote to all the parents telling them we could close by the end of September and included a letter for them to sign and send to councillors. There has been a fantastic response and this is great news for the Boys' Club".

The council grant was vital to help meet the running costs of the club. Councillor Stephen Byers, deputy leader of North Tyneside Council said there was wide spread concern over the future of the club.

Councillor Muriel Green, chairman of the council's education committee, responsible for grants to youth organisations said, "We recognised the importance of this Boys' Club".

Sunday Sun 15th June 1997.

1997 saw dismay expressed by Peter Kirkley, then working for Middlesbrough Football Club, about what he saw as the wreck of the Youth Development policy at Newcastle United. He was quoted extensively in the press criticising the man who sacked him, Tyneside legend Kevin Keegan, for destroying a youth policy once envied across the land. The Magpies fanatic first discovered a chubby 12-year-old called Paul Gascoigne for Newcastle, along with first team players Robbie Elliott, Steve Watson, Lee Clark and England defender Steve Howie. But despite a superb track record for spotting and developing young stars Peter and his assistant Stan Nixon were kicked out by Keegan, just three months into his St. James's Park reign. Five years on, Peter insisted the conveyor belt had dried up at United, and that his new club Middlesbrough were beginning to reap the benefits by beating the Geordie giants to the cream of the North East's young talent. And he was left in no doubt who was to blame.

"I know that Stan and I had done a good job with the kids at Newcastle, but Keegan wasn't broad minded enough to give us a chance", said Kirkley.

"Keegan came in and said youth policy was not his priority. Keegan did a lot of brilliant things for Newcastle United, but on this, he was wrong, and I told him so. What happened to the youth policy at Newcastle was very sad. The Keegan hype swayed a lot of heads at first and meant United got their pick of

TOP CLASS . . . Kirkley's United finds include, from top, Gazza, Steve Howey, Steve Watson and Robbie Elliott.

Sunday Sun 15th June 1997.

the talent, but now a lot of the lads are starting to ask, where am I going to go now. There is a big gap between the first team and the youngsters, and there's no one of the quality of Watson, Clark and Elliott coming through".

Peter's argument was backed up by the news that the England squad for the World Youth Cup in Malaysia later that month contained two players each from Manchester United, Liverpool and Arsenal, but none from St. James's.

"What Keegan didn't accept was that you still need a solid base, even with the chequebook. As far as youth is concerned, I don't think there's much left for Kenny Dalglish to build on, and it took me four or five years to build up the conveyor belt last time. The good 16, 17 and 18 year olds have gone elsewhere and Dalglish has to look abroad for youngsters".

Despite the millions spent by Keegan, United's squad still lacked strength in depth, as was shown when Dalglish had to put young Paul Barrett on the bench for a UEFA Cup quarter final in Monaco.

(Peter later returned to Newcastle United as its Youth Development Officer and in 2003 was elected President of Wallsend Boys' Club.)

Girls muscling in on Boys' Club

The Journal, Wednesday February 4, 1998.

In 1998 Wallsend Boys' Club again faced the issue of whether or not to give girls full membership. It was decided that the time had come for this to happen. Forty female members were recruited which was a tiny proportion of a club with nearly 900 members.

For years boys had been the traditional members of the organisation. But the club was aware that women and girls were getting more interested in sports, particularly those like rugby and football, which were once considered a male only domain.

But although club officials wanted to extend membership to include more girls, they said they had not yet got the facilities to accommodate them at the 42-year-old clubhouse.

It was felt right to keep the name Wallsend Boys' Club, and to stay part of the National Association of Boys' Clubs, in spite of having female members. Funds were then needed for an overhaul of the club's furnishings and facilities. £500,000 was estimated by Dave Beardall as being needed, but the plans included being able to open up the club even more to the community.

Exiled Geordie lads Jonathan Douglas and Chris Atkinson returned home in August 1998 to play with excess baggage.

The pair, from North Tyneside, brought their American University football team with them to play in pre-season games in the North East. Jonathan and Chris both played for Wallsend Boys' Club and Northumberland Schools prior to gaining scholarships at Quincy University, Illinois. They were then in their final year at university.

The Quincy football team brought some of their supporters with them. It was nice for Jonathan and Chris to have some support from their fellow Geordies.

In the September worried mum Monica Guthrey appealed to the Boys' Club to ban smoking.

Monica feared youngsters at Wallsend Boys' Club were getting the wrong message because they saw adults smoking in the club.

She believed the sight of parents, committee members and over-16s smoking, would encourage juniors to try cigarettes.

Her eldest son Matthew, aged 10, played for the junior team and her other son Jack, 5, was also a member of the club.

"There is no justification for a youth club to allow smoking; it surely goes against what they are about.

I have nothing against people who want to smoke, but I feel doing it in front of kids is not only inappropriate, it is selfish. Clubs like this have a major influence on youngsters", said Monica.

Club leader David Beardall said, "Not many people actually smoke at the club, but it is something we are looking into."

Within twelve months smoking was totally banned on the Boys' Club premises.

In the same month Sunderland star Lee Clark went back to his roots to accept Northumbrian Water's sponsorship of the football section for Wallsend Boys' Club. And it was a big day also for the four promising youngsters who were picked to accept the £1,000 football shaped cheque alongside Lee.

FUMING MAD – Monica Guthery, whose sons Matthew and Jack are members of the club

Evening Chronicle September 10th 1998.

Lee was on the injured list with a broken leg in plaster. He said, "This club set me and other top players on the right road, and sponsorship like this from Northumbrian Water is so important as the future of the club depends on it".

Wallsend Boys' Club, was back in the limelight on 16th October as a "Memory lane" location for Alan Shearer's TV commercial for McDonald's.

The Newcastle striker, filmed a scene at the Boys' Club with his mentor, the veteran football scout Jack Hixon, and states in the TV voice-over,

"This is where I got my real education". Alan had turned up at seven in the morning with a vast film crew of 48, they'd been filming since first light at the shipyard, and they shot some early scenes before the supporting cast of 40 Boys' club footballers turned up half an hour later.

Alan Shearer with Jack Hixon during the making of the McDonalds advert at Wallsend Boys' Club.

David Beardall, the club leader said, "It's always good to have positive publicity for Wallsend and the Boys' club movement in general".

It could have been a difficult day though. The Wallsend scenes were shot the morning after the infamous match against Sunderland in which Alan had been relegated to the substitute's bench. The first lad through the door came straight out with the inevitable question, "Alan, what's it like to be dropped".

David Beardall said he flinched when he heard that one, although the famously impassive Shearer, who played up to his "boring"image in the McDonald's advert, didn't bat an eyelid. He just looked out the window, and said, "It's a nice day outside, isn't it."

However, the England skipper did have to make an early exit that morning and left Wallsend Boys' Club at ten to nine, on the dot, when a chauffeur driven Jaguar came to pick him up. The Wallsend Old Boy grimly remarked that he didn't want to be late for training with Ruud Gullit. But that, of course, is another story.

In 1998 another Old Boy was honoured in his new home town of Boston, Massachusetts.
In 1994, Nick Bone, one of the club's footballers, had won a soccer scholarship to the USA.

The young "Geordie" was honoured by being named amongst the top 20 athletes of the century produced by Boston University in America. Nick, a former pupil at St. Cuthbert's Grammar School in Newcastle, was ranked 10th in the list of Boston all-time greats.

Nick was a soccer player whose achievements on the American University circuit smashed several records. His citation on his selection reads, "During the 50 year history of the Boston University men's soccer Nick Bone was the driving force on four of the best teams to play at Nickerson Field.

Nick in 1998 was the impetus of a terrier squad that won five straight America East titles and earned five straight N.C.A.A. Tournament appearances.

During his four years Nick started all 84 games and became the second player ever to earn All-Conference, all four seasons. Nick is the Terriers all-time leading scorer with 61 goals. He was named America East Tournaments most outstanding player in 1996 and 1997 and was also named Soccer America's freshman of the Year in 1994 when he set Boston's single season record of 18 goals."

He later played semi-pro football for Cape Cod where he was inevitably top scorer in his first season.

Victorious boys' club team devastated by raid for their gear
Soccer kids are hit by kit thieves

As the 20th century came to a close, the club was clearly looking to the future whilst being determined to remember and celebrate its past. Sadly however, the year 2000 got off to a bad start for WBC.

In January the local papers reported that some of the budding soccer stars were facing a chilly winter because thieves had stolen their kit.

The under-15s players at Wallsend Boys' Club were stunned when criminals walked off with an entire match set. The under 15s who were top of their league with a 100 per cent record were now being forced to beg and borrow unless they could get their strips back.

The raiders broke into the garage of a member of staff in Killingworth and made off with a set of 18 kits, sweat shirts and footballs.

Team manager Brian Selby said, "It's devastating at this time of the year when we are halfway through the season and doing so well". The kits were very distinctive, yellow tops with Wallsend Boys' Club printed on them, along with the White Swan white motif on the chest, white shorts and green socks. The dark green sweatshirts also had the white Swan emblem.

The Crime prevention officer from Wallsend police station said "This was a callous crime, depriving the kids from the Boys' club".

By the beginning of the 21st century Wallsend Boys' Club was probably stronger than ever in terms of success and spirit, but financial pressures continued.

Dave Beardall was quoted in interviews in April 2001 pointing out that WBC had received nothing from any Football Club in return for the players they had produced. His comments came as a TV documentary presented by BBC pundit Alan Hansen revealed the going rate for a 10-year-old child prodigy was an astonishing £50,000.

But while Premiership clubs splashed out whopping fees on the next generation of soccer starlets, grassroots amateur teams got nothing.

Kevin Bell, one of the 11-a-side team managers of Wallsend Boys' Club, revealed how the only incentive in his time has been a set of kit when Peter Beardsley joined Carlisle. And this is despite producing an astonishing array of professional talent. The season 2000/2001 had been a record-breaking year for the club after six players, were signed by professional clubs. Kevin Bell said, "If a team signed one of our players and the club gave us £500 it would be a bonus". Graeme Carrick, brother of West Ham star Michael, who also played for the Boys' club, and Phil Lumsden had both gone to West Ham. The other lads were going to Bolton, Blackburn, Wimbledon and Hibernian.

Kevin Bell.

Kevin hoped that Newcastle United would help out in the future after the club contributed £5,000 to rival amateur team Walker Central. The money was to fund a development plan for the club responsible for the Toon striker Shola Ameobi.

Kevin said, "One season Newcastle United signed four of our players, Lee Clark, Alan Thompson, Steve Watson and Robbie Elliott. That is four of our players who have brought Newcastle millions in the transfer market. We are delighted for Walker and wonder if Newcastle will carry on doing it".

The BBC documentary 'Football's Dream Factory' looked at how the top professional clubs were signing players as young as six. Former Scotland defender Alan Hansen said, "To get the best kids the football clubs themselves are offering huge incentives.

We did not really go into figures in the programme, but there are a couple of managers who told us the money involved was quite substantial".

But despite his team missing out, Kevin Bell remained philosophical. He said,"Our main aim objective is to get them off the streets, to be truthful. To try and make them better people and if they become professional footballers then that's a bonus".

One of the first new developments of the new century was a Club website which was launched in February 2002. In October 2002 former members who were now soccer stars were proving they had not forgotten their football roots.

Players past and present were pouring out tributes to Wallsend Boys' Club where they first honed their skills, by helping them launch the clubs first Internet website.

David Beardall, club leader, said, "We set up the website in February and wrote to the players asking for a few words.

Most of our ex players who have turned pro do keep in touch and are highly respected by all the lads at the club.

They are genuinely grateful for the footballing start they had and it is nice to see they still remember us fondly".

In spite of what appeared to be a lack of appreciation by the big Football Club institutions, as has been seen, the individual players who progressed from the Boys' Club remain faithful and show great loyalty to their roots.

This tradition continues with the latest star, Michael Carrick, then playing for Tottenham, who sponsors the under-8s five-a-side league. In May 2002, when he was recovering from surgery on an injury, he visited the club to present prizes to the next generation of young players.
"I joined the Boys' Club when I was five and played for them until I went to West Ham at 16".

Michael Carrick sponsors U8 League

By 2003, the club was also trying to respond to a growing interest among the girls of the area in playing football. Thanks to Barbara Parker, whose children had long been coming to the Boys' Club, volunteering as a referee, the first girls match took place in May of that year.

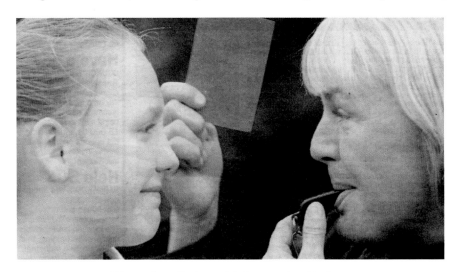

Player Amy Parker with her mother Barbara.

In 2003 Wallsend Boys' Club started its first ever girls' eleven-a-side team, which was a major break through for girls in a male dominated club.

The girl's team proved to be very successful and they intend to increase the number of female teams at the club in future years.

The first girls team at Wallsend Boys' Club, attend the football presentation night 2006.

Chapter 12 - Celebrations and Memories

A very significant development in the Club was a change of leadership. Dave Beardall had been appointed back in December 1965, before the building was even open for business, and he had led the club ever since, which was a remarkable achievement.

By October 2003 however, at the age of 65, his retirement came, marked with a lavish celebration at a local hotel. Among other tributes paid to Dave was the very first presentation of the Barclaycard Premiership 'Free Kicks Champion Award' newly introduced for those who had made outstanding contributions to grassroots football. This was presented to Dave by Peter Beardsley. Among the wealth of memories shared by Dave that evening was the fact that the first ever match played by a club team after its opening in 1966 ended in a 21-0 defeat for the club.

What a lesson in not being discouraged! On the same evening presentations were made to Joe Kirtley, who was retiring from his position as club president, and Bob Slone, who had worked as a volunteer for 35 years with 5-a-side teams.

As can be seen from the accounts of their contributions written up for the occasion, both by the local press and club committee, this event really did mark the end of a whole era for Wallsend Boys' Club.

Official Retirement Evening at the Village Hotel.

David Beardall. Club Leader.

Joe Kirtley. Club President.

Robert Slone. Voluntary Coach

David Beardall.

A host of football stars owe their glittering array of medals and trophies to unsung hero David Beardall and David now finally receives his own reward for his services to soccer at Wallsend Boys' Club. Premiership sponsors Barclaycard awarded him with their very first Free Kicks Champion Award in honour of his 37 years in grass roots football. Former Newcastle United and England legend Peter Beardsley, who started his career with the Boys' Club, presented the award in a ceremony at the club.

Youth worker Dave has overseen the development of the club's football committee since 1965, helping to produce top players like Alan Shearer, Lee Clark, Steve Watson, Alan Thompson, Robbie Elliott and Michael Carrick. The club has provided leisure activities for youngsters in the area since 1938 but has been at its present site since 1965.

"Our aim is to give kids the opportunity to fill their free time in a safe environment, when I'm sure otherwise some would be involved in anti-social behaviour".

David Beardall walked into Wallsend Boys' Club in 1965; it's real birth as a centre of football excellence. Yet the first match he arranged ended in a 21-0 defeat. "Oh, I remember it all right", David said, wincing. "We played St. Mary's Boys' Club at Cowgate roundabout and got slaughtered. I begged the ref to whistle up five minutes early". From embarrassment a great and mighty club emerged.

The growth of Wallsend Boys' Club was so rapid that David soon realised he couldn't run the club and its soccer teams, so he asked Peter Kirkley to take over the football section and it was one of the best decisions that David ever made.

David with Northumberland Association of Boys' Clubs County Secretary Nigel Voules.

Dave retired from a full time job after 38 years of hard work, loyalty and dedication. He was 65 years old on 7th October and 24 hours later he was honoured at a lavish dinner before many of his superstar protégés. He has been a father figure, a mentor to those destined for superstardom and those not, and his memories will be treasured well into his thoroughly deserved leisure time. Memories like the time Steve Watson, the youngest ever Newcastle United debutant, acted as a corner man at the Henry Cooper Golden Belt boxing competition which was held at the Boys' Club and was televised on Channel Four.

Another occasion, which saw Peter Beardsley, gifted enough to become an England legend, taken one Thursday night to Newcastle United when the apprentices were training by David Young who played for Newcastle and also coached at the Boys' Club. But Beardsley was rejected because he was too small. It was ridiculous. Peter had three eyes, one left, one right and one in the back of his head. He was a mesmerising player, so gifted. He also had natural eye to ball coordination. After Newcastle eventually got Peter from Vancouver Whitecaps, Peter came down to the club and had a game of pool. Dave said, "He played a shot that was so outrageous and I told him that it was a fluke. So he did it again. That was Peter, a genius".

Recollections, too, of the numerous trips David made with Birmingham City boss Steve Bruce, one time captain of Manchester United's championship winners, picking him up from school to rush him to Boys' Club games. Steve was the best player never to be capped by England.

His advice to rookie goalkeeper Eric Steele was to be "more like Jack Fairbrother". "I remember going to watch Eric play one of his early games for Newcastle Reserves.

Bob Moncur was coming back from injury and he gave Eric a right rollicking for not commanding his box. Bob took a full-blooded whack in the nuts and went down like a sack of spuds. He really sorted out Eric; I could hear every word standing behind the goal".

"Not so long ago I did some TV with Michael Carrick, it was for Sky. When it was shown, Steve Bruce was in the studio." "Hey, that's David Beardall", he said. "The old devil is still at Wallsend Boys' Club, I owe him a lot". That really pleased me.

David chuckles at them all, peering over his half rimmed spectacles and taking a huge drag on his cigarette. "Oh, I haven't made much money but I wouldn't change my life for anything. Its been wonderfully rewarding".

Rummaging in a drawer for a photograph he finally produces it with a triumphant flourish. It's of Lee Clark in a Sunderland strip.

"I asked Lee to sign it when he was here at the end of last season so we could frame it but he wouldn't", laughed Dave. "I think it was something to do with the colour of the stripes". Lee still comes down to the Boys' Club, he watches his nephew play, who is in one of our teams.

Alan Thompson came to the gala dinner and got a taxi back up to Glasgow. David said proudly, "He should have been in the England side, they've cried out for a left sided player but because Alan is playing in Scotland he's been overlooked."

Alan Shearer presenting David Beardall with a retirement gift at the Village Hotel.

David Beardall has never received the headlines that some of his protégés have enjoyed. He is unsung like so many who have devoted their life to grass roots football. However, Dave was centre stage at his retirement and the likes of Shearer, Beardsley, Watson, Thompson, Elliott, Clark and Carrick were the chorus boys.

"I'm terrified", he said. "I go cold at the thought".

(After his retirement David has continued to help at the Boys' Club in a volunteer role, this is the true mark of a man committed to the development of children).

Joe Kirtley was a self employed Haulage and Coal Merchant through the 1960s, 70's and 80's and during that time has been a great friend of David Beardall through their golfing association.

In 1970 Joe was asked by David to join Wallsend Boys' Club in a voluntary capacity as a patron and to sit on the committee. At this time there were about five to ten members on the committee. Over the last three decades Joe's help has been invaluable.

With his wealth of knowledge and wisdom he has helped to structure and maintain the boys club through the 70's, 80's and 90's.

Joe was soon appointed President of Wallsend Boys' Club, and with a firm grip steered the club into the new Millennium.

Joe Kirtley.

Joe has attended and run many functions on behalf of Wallsend Boys' Club and one of his greatest memories was that of Henry Cooper's Golden Belt boxing series, which was televised in the early 1980s with Henry Cooper in attendance.

Joe often has a smile when he remembers a certain young lad at Wallsend Boys' Club, New Years Eve, party in the 90's. The young lad was assisting and waiting on the top table and surrounding tables in the hall. When he was asked to make sure that he was not neglecting any of the other tables around, he replied, "You must be bloody joking, I'm getting 50p tip off this table for every round, I ain't moving from here".

That young lad was Steve Watson.

Joe has been a marvellous servant to Wallsend Boys' Club supporting all the junior members and their activities throughout his many years with the club and will be greatly missed after his retirement.

Robert Slone had worked at Wallsend Boys' Club on a voluntary basis for over 35 years running 5-a-side teams, 11-a-side teams and doing coaching sessions at the Boys' Club for two hours every Saturday evening.

This is where the youngest members of the Boys' club come into the game with Robert's help and guidance.

Robert Slone.

Robert was a professional footballer (goalkeeper) in Scotland in his early days, and over the years he has retained his connections with the local teams by taking his own eleven-a-side teams to play in week long tournaments in Edinburgh and Nottingham, with players ranging from seven to thirteen years of age.

This was hard work indeed, as the budding superstars never seemed to sleep and high jinks such as room raids by the players was often their way of stopping Robert and his helpers get any sleep at all during the tours.

He ran these excursions for over twenty-five years. He was very much involved in the early development of players such as Steve Watson, Alan Thompson and Michael Carrick who played in his famous "Brazilian" 5-a-side teams. Robert will always be remembered at the Boys' Club for his "Brazilian 5-a-side teams".

We later saw his former players bringing their children along to Robert's Saturday sessions, with as many as seventy young budding footballers (including girls) taking part.

Steve Watson presenting Robert with a Brazil shirt signed by his former players Alan Thompson, Michael Carrick and Steve Watson at the Village Hotel.

Pele presenting a Brazil shirt signed by him, to Wallsend Boys' Club chairman Steve Dale with Michael Daley on the right.The shirt raised nearly £5000 for the Boys' club, in auction at David Beardall's retirement evening.

In May 2003 Robert received the recognition he totally deserved when, at Wallsend Town Hall; he was awarded the Chair of North Tyneside's Commendation Award, for outstanding service to the community.

He has also been awarded a number of Keystone awards from the Northumberland Association of Clubs for Young People including the rarely awarded Platinum certificate.

Long serving volunteers to the community are few and far between and Robert has been a star in this field. His dedication and enthusiasm over the years has been relentless and his desire to see young footballing talent develop has been second to none. Robert has been a true ambassador for Wallsend Boys' Club for over thirty-five years and is a great miss to the club.

Mid 2003 saw the appointment of Garry Marshall, as Wallsend Boys' Club's new Leader, with Marc Nash appointed as his assistant. Garry was ready to bring in his own ideas and innovations to ensure the club remained a potent force. One of these ideas was the further development of the web site and the establishment of an Internet café in one of the upper rooms in the club building. Garry hoped that this would encourage young members to combine their visits to the club for training and socialising with opportunities to complete their homework for school. The upstairs room was also equipped with an interactive whiteboard to support theoretical training sessions taking place there.

Internet Café at Wallsend Boys' Club

Martial Arts have for many years, been an important and popular activity at Wallsend Boys' Club. With both adults and children taking part in this demanding and fulfilling activity.

Shinnosuke Murata (centre) and Yoichiro Kawamura (right).

The following year Wallsend Boys' Club found themselves with some players from way outside the 5 mile limit.

Move over Alan Shearer and Peter Beardsley, meet Wallsend Boys' Club's latest signings, in 2004 15 year olds Shinnosuke Murata and Yoichiro Kawamura from Japan were desperate to make their mark on the English map at the legendary football factory. Goalkeeper Shinnosuke, whose hero is David Seaman, and Yoichiro, a centre back, both play for the academy side of Shonan Bellmare in their homeland. Even though this club has brought through seven Japanese internationals, including World Cup star Hidetoshi Nakata, the boys had set their sights on the Premiership.

Shinnosuke's father, Mayako Murata, was quoted in the press as saying, "Although the boys will be playing football in the youth category, they both have desires of playing in England. This is because we feel that the under-15 players in Japan, Europe and South America are not so different from each other; the elder players seem very different in their performances. We think this could be caused by the differences in the methods of training between these countries and Japan. As a result, the lads want to increase their skills through playing in a strong youth team in England".

After finding out that restrictions on the number of non-EU players would rule out the chance of playing for a top Premiership academy side, they resolved the situation by finding a suitable youth team who could take them on.

"It was made clear to us that England have organisations called Boys' Clubs, which are as good as academies. Indeed Wallsend has produced a lot of players, so we believed the club would make Shinnosuke and Yoichiro the better players that they wanted to be". Wallsend Boys' Club leader Garry Marshall had agreed to the lads flying in from Japan to Tyneside, to see if they were good enough to make the grade. But the main obstacle standing in their way was the difficulty of getting a visa allowing them to go to school and play football in England. Garry had no intention of letting any potential Eastern promise slip through his fingers. He said, "We haven't got the resources to help with their schooling, but if they want to come in the summer, and they're good enough, we'll certainly take them on".

Wallsend Boys' Clubs under-11's and under-15's teams flew off to the U.S.A. in the summer of 2004 to take part in an international football tournament. The teams won the Disney International Cup; the first time two teams from the UK had won at the prestigious event.

Wallsend Boys' Club under 11's team with Kicks FC in Orlando 2004.

After months of meticulous planning and fund raising, the two teams made the journey across the Atlantic. Around £25,000 was needed to make the trip possible, and the target was met just two weeks before the departure date. Both teams were impressive throughout the group stages, winning their three games to qualify for the final phase despite temperatures in the high 90's.

Remaining unbeaten throughout, both sides found themselves in their respective finals and won.

Garry Marshall said, "It was an excellently-run tournament. The American people were very impressed with our standard both on and off the pitch and our visit had given them a strong indication of the direction they wanted to take their own junior football".

Garry also mentioned that Michael McMullen, who was too old to play in the under-11 age group, had got fixed up to play for the Californian Wildcats in the under-13's age group and had an excellent time.

Under 15 coach Alan Jarvis added, "It was a trip of a lifetime and a fitting finale to a lot of hard work by the club".

Wallsend Boys' Club thanked fund raising organiser Karen Crammond, the players, their parents and all the local sponsors who made the trip possible.

Both these events seemed to be a reflection of the changing times, with a more global context for the club than would have been deemed possible back in 1938, or even 1966.

Wallsend Boys' Club under 15's with Ajax Orlando 2004.

November 2004. The National Association Of Clubs for Young People along with the Amateur Boxing Association held their prestigious National Semi-Finals: - North & Scotland versus Midlands & Northern Ireland.

The event consisted of twenty-three bouts divided into three age groups.
Class A: 15 years of age; Class B: 16 years of age; and Class C: 17-19 years of age.
Michael McGill, one of the band of helpers on the day, described it all later.

"The day started early, 8am for some of the volunteers. The marquee company came and the enthusiastic volunteers started to lay the special carpet down over the five a side pitch, so that when the boxing ring was erected it wouldn't damage the playing area.

They then headed up to the café and started to make up 150 packed lunches for the contestants and their seconds. With a mini production line of six people buttering bread, making fillings, making and wrapping the sandwiches etc. Then to their dismay the contestants and their followers started arriving early, at 9.30am. But the weighing in time wasn't until 1pm and the tournament wasn't due to start until 2.30pm.

Breakfasts, hot sandwiches and hot drinks for the guests were now suddenly a priority, with some of the volunteers also diverted to the "Boxing Arena" where a couple of hundred seats had to be laid out around the boxing ring which was being constructed in the middle of the hall.

The café helpers were now running at one hundred and fifty per cent and had to send out for more supplies, with the bar, now also doing very good business. In the judo room the boxers were now weighing in and warming up, when a mini crisis occurred, as the running water suddenly stopped, and water had to be brought into the club in containers from a nearby house.

The twenty-three bouts ran off well although in one fight both contestants were disqualified, and a few bloody noses were all that some boxers received for their efforts. At 7.30pm the tournament was over, but for the wrecked volunteers the enormous job of cleaning up the mess, removing the seats, dismantling the ring etc was just starting. By 9pm they were able to retire to the bar for a quick drink before going home for a well-earned nights sleep. The boxing tournament was a huge success with the winners going on to compete at St. Paul's Amateur Boxing Club in Hull."

In 2005 more welcome sponsorship was received when Paul Rogers and Gary Williams of Unika donated a brand new 17-seater top of the range mini-bus to the Boys' Club.

During the year the club committee were much involved with preparations for the grand celebration to mark the 40th anniversary of the 'new' (but now quite old), club building.

As part of those celebrations it was decided that it would be great to document as much of the club's history as possible. In order to help with that research Michael McGill and Vince Carrick, who were at the heart of the 'Heritage Project, made a plea in the local press for information from any former members of the original club to help in their research. The plea was successful and interviews with former members started to take place.

It was soon realised in interviews with five of the veteran former members, Jack Scott, James McBlain, Fred Tate, Ray Oliver and Jimmy Swan, that over FIFTY YEARS earlier these gentlemen had been good friends with each other. Through the passing of time, changing jobs etc, they had not been in contact with each other for many years. On 6th March 2005 Michael and Vince re-united the five gentlemen at Wallsend Boys' Club.

Jack Scott, 78, a retired British Gas engineer born in Wallsend and now living in Forest Hall, joined the Boys' Club as a 15 year old and had not been back since the 1950's. "I've got some great memories of this place. It was a good group of lads", he said. "It was like a second home to me, but as we all got into our early 20's we drifted apart".

James McBlain, 78, of Hadrian Park, Wallsend, joined as a 12 year old in 1938 and went on to become President of the club in 1969.

Mr McBlain, a retired instrument curator at the Dental Hospital at Newcastle's RVI, said "We were young and just looking for somewhere to play football and do other sports or hobbies to keep ourselves out of trouble".

Fred Tate, 78, of Holy Cross, Wallsend, who was an engineer at Swan Hunter and Parsons, spent a lot of his time working on pantomimes and plays at the club. "We would put plays on and compete against other clubs", he said. "I've got a lot of great memories and it's really good to see all these people again. It's the first time I've been here since the 40's".

Ray Oliver, 78. of Wallsend, was there from 1938 to 1952 and was a top gymnast and a PT instructor. "It's really good to come back", he said. "There are a lot of good memories of this place".

Jimmy Swan, 69, formerly of Wallsend but now living in North Shields began attending the Boys' club in 1949 as a 12 year-old. He said, "I played football here and was a centre forward. I used to come to the Boys' club a few years ago with my grandson as well, and he loved it".

Bringing together these grand gentlemen after fifty years apart, and to then to re-kindle their friendships was seen as a massive bonus to the authors in the research for this book.

The coverage of the reunion in the Evening Chronicle led to another contact being made. The Chronicle's article included a picture of the Old Boys' football team from the early 50's, prompting an unexpected call from Canada on behalf of David Henderson.

Relations in Newcastle who thought they recognised him on the photograph contacted Mr Henderson, who emigrated in 1970. Speaking from London, Ontario, the 70 year-old said, "What a pleasant surprise it was to see the photograph, I played for Wallsend Boys' Club for a couple of seasons from 1950. Some of the pitches we played on in those days left a lot to be desired. When we played away to Willington Quay Boys' Club the pitch was on an old rubbish dump and if a player came into contact with the ground he generally got cut from cinders or pieces of glass.

Our home pitch was on West Street, which meant we had to walk from the Boys' Club on Station Road through the allotments at the back of the Boys' club in our football strips. We enjoyed playing so this was no hardship to us. We trained on Wednesday nights in the

Dave Henderson in the 1950's and now.

club hall. I remember the club leader "Sandy"; he used to take the part of the dame in the pantomimes. I must say the photograph brought back a lot of memories of happy times".

And back to the 21st century, two weeks later on 21st March, Alan Shearer and Michael Carrick, both products of Wallsend Boys' Club lined up against each other in the FA Cup quarter final tie at St. James's Park.

Michael said, "I grew up worshipping Alan as a player because of what he meant to Newcastle. I know how much he wants to win something this season, but as a Geordie myself, I'd love to see him win something this year, but we want to win the FA Cup. He can have the UEFA Cup. Alan's a legend up at Newcastle and deserves to be. He's the greatest scorer in the Premier League. A quarter final of the FA Cup is always huge but for me to go back home is special".

In the summer of 2005 in preparation for the coming season a code of conduct / behaviour scheme was launched at the club for the representative teams. This led the way on high standards of behaviour on and off the pitch and was backed by the club managers and parents. It received national coverage in the press, on radio and on television, showing the club tackling this important issue.

After months of planning and preparation, October 6th 2005 saw Wallsend Boys' Club celebrate the 40th anniversary of the 'new club' opening for business. And what a celebration it was!

Millions of pounds worth of footballing talent crammed into the Marriott Gosforth Park Hotel to pay tribute to their roots at the club.

Newcastle United skipper Alan Shearer and Peter Beardsley headed the sparkling guest list but there were plenty more of the game's stars in attendance during this latest chapter of one football's amazing success stories. 'Toon' players Lee Clark and Robbie Elliott were joined by former United team-mates Steve Watson, and Celtic favourite Alan Thompson. However the list did not end there with Tottenham Hotspur and England's Michael Carrick chauffeured up to Tyneside from North London to meet up with old friends and colleagues.

Michael said, "I had a good night, it was great to come back and say thank you to people. Wallsend was where it all started for me and I will always be grateful to everybody at the club who helped give me a start in the game". Tony Sealy, ex-QPR, travelled from Hong Kong to be here. Also on show were another 23 first team professional footballers: -

Paul Baker, Southampton, Steve Baker, Southampton, Ian Bogie, Newcastle United, Phil Cavener, Burnley, Tony Dinning, Newcastle United, Chris Hedworth, Newcastle United, Russell Irving, Ipswich Town, Gary Leonard, West Bromwich Albion, Paul Malcolm, Newcastle United, Kevin McDonald, Hibernian, Marc

Nash, Hartlepool United, Phil Ray, Burnley, David Robinson, Newcastle United, Geoff smith, Burnley, Eric Steele, Newcastle United, Paul Stephenson, Newcastle United, Mick Tait, Portsmouth, Jeff Tate, Burnley, Barrie Wardrobe, Sunderland, Mick Wardrobe, Burnley, Ian Watson, Sunderland, John Watson, Newcastle United and Jeff Wrightson, Newcastle United.

Barry Hindson of BBC radio Newcastle, said he was fortunate to be a guest at the social event of the week, which celebrated forty years of Wallsend Boys' Club. A veritable host of footballing talent, which served its formative years at the Station Road club, were in attendance, as well as good friends including Stuart Leason from the NFA, the evergreen and magnificent Jack Hixon, and the manager of Bedlington Terriers, Keith Perry.

With respect to those fine gentlemen though, this was Wallsend Boys' Club's night in every sense and when Peter Kirkley introduced the former club members, what a roll of honour it was.

And after the meal Alan Shearer, Peter Beardsley, Michael Carrick and Alan Thompson all joined forces to take part in a question and answer session with the audience.

At the Dinner Garry Marshall spoke movingly of the more general work of the Boys' Club, and of its mission, not to produce professional footballers, but to help every member make the most of themselves.

The Club chairman, Steve Dale echoed those sentiments in his speech, which seemed to sum up the huge achievement of the club, but also the challenges facing it. He said:

"Twenty years of experience working in the financial services industry has instilled in me the following warning for my clients, **'Past performances should not be relied upon as a guide to future performance.'**
So, after forty years that has seen the Club produce over 60 professional footballers, 6 of which went on to represent England, Canada and New Zealand at international level, maintaining that 'past

performance' is a daunting challenge for the Club. There are far more youth football clubs competing with us for players and professional club Academies are inviting players to join them at an earlier age. However, Wallsend Boys' Club has never been just about providing professional footballers. The fact that the club gained such an enviable reputation for this ability has actually been a welcome by-product of striving to fulfil the founding members' objectives, enshrined in the guiding Constitution of the Club.
"The objectives of the Club are to help and educate members through leisure activities to develop their physical, mental and spiritual capacity in order to help them become useful and responsible members of society."

Judged on these objectives, the production line from Wallsend Boys' Club runs into tens of thousands, and that is the reason the Club still generates deep affection from ex-members. These ex-members and their talents are not only woven into the fabric of the game of football, but also the corridors of political power and civil service, the cut and thrust of business, the caring professions, the bright lights of the entertainment industry, the arts, and all points in between. Alan Shearer got to Wembley with his football boots, Gordon Sumner got there with his bass guitar.

Indications show that Mr G. B. Hunter, M.D. of Swan Hunter shipyard gave birth to the Club at the turn of the last century, to provide their apprentices with a positive outlet for their energies. Mr Hunter could scarcely have imagined that those humble beginnings would be the start of an organisation that would evolve into a magnetic hub for the football-loving youth of Tyneside. That is what has happened. For a hundred years, successive generations of Tynesiders have used the Club to play football, star in pantomimes, gymnastics, taking part and watching boxing tournaments, learn martial arts, celebrate birthdays, meet their mates and generally put the world to rights. The Club has been a sanctuary for all those activities. None of them could have spent that quality time with their grandparents, parents, brothers, sisters, or mates, if it had not been for the selfless effort of our successive generations of volunteers.

To grasp the scale of that effort, try to imagine a school with over 1,000 pupils. Now try to imagine that this school does not just have a typical daily timetable, it remains open for the unsocial hours, every weekday evening and all weekends. Finally, try to imagine that this school does not pay the fifty "Teachers" it has for these unsocial hours and you will begin to understand the enormity of the effort that goes into running this Club by our team managers, referees, fundraisers, management committee and other volunteers. This landmark evening is a celebration of the wonderful generosity of these individuals over the last century.

So what of the next forty years? We cannot guarantee to produce 3 professional footballers every 2 years, but don't bet against it! However, we can guarantee to provide a home for all those relationships that have been so important to the youth of Tyneside in the past. Our existing home is going through a mid-life crisis and looking all 480 months of age. To remain an attractive home for our members, we desperately need to bring our facilities into the 21st century, so we are currently discussing our options with North Tyneside Council. Ideally we would like to build a new club facility, with enough pitches for our 16 representative teams. It is remarkable that the representative teams have achieved what they have done over the years, without their own pitches. North Tyneside Council "brought the boys home" for the start of this season and we are very grateful to them for putting us back on our own patch. They also brought the girls home; last year saw the launch of our first representative girls' team, who did us all proud coming third in their league and runners-up in a Cup Final. We intend to considerably expand the number of our representative teams, with a "cradle to grave" philosophy. Starting an under-18 team, an adult side, and more girls teams are key priorities for the next two seasons.

It all cost time and money. Despite the unprecedented amount of money flowing to the game of football today, we rely heavily upon the continued goodwill and support of North Tyneside Council, Northumberland Football Association, and our kind business sponsors and grant providers. Also our ex-players generously give their time for occasions and we are sure they will continue to give whatever support they can in the future. If you would like to help us make the future vision a reality, call the Club. Together we can all continue to deliver on the Club's Constitution."

Wallsend Boys Club.
40th Anniversary. October 2005

Chapter 13 – Onwards and Upwards: Not quite the Final Word

In many ways the celebration of October 2005 would seem to be an ideal place to stop the History of Wallsend Boys' Club, forty years into existence in the 'new' clubhouse on Station Road. There was, and is still much to come however as will be seen from this brief summary of the years between 2005 and 2013.

The club's sporting activities continued to develop with further boxing competitions, Judo and even street dance. For the first time in many years a senior football team was formed in 2007, winning success the following year in a competition in Rogatz celebrating the centenary of the SV Concordia club there – the same one which Bob Corkhill had close associations with.

Links to former players continued with Michael Carrick, newly transferred to Manchester United, presenting new strips to all 19 Boys' Club teams in 2006. In the same year Peter Beardsley officially opened a new Astroturf pitch to replace the old maple floor which had been damaged by flooding.

As the Chairman had indicated in his speech at the 2005 dinner however, sport was not the only focus for the Club. Work continued with efforts to transform the lives of local young people in other ways. The 'Positive Futures' scheme was taken on by the club, and the 'Boyza Bus' offered the opportunity to reach out to young people in other parts of North Tyneside.

Recognition for this, and all the other good work carried out by the club over the decades, came in 2007 when the club was awarded Freedom of the Borough. At the ceremony to confer the award Councillor Jim Allan referred to the club as a 'jewel in the community'.

The motion to award the Freedom of the Borough said:

"This honour is in recognition of the outstanding achievements made by Wallsend Boys' Club, in providing an important and long lasting community resource for the young people of Wallsend and beyond. The Boys' club have been exemplary ambassadors for our region, producing stars such as Michael Carrick, Alan Shearer, Peter Beardsley and many others on the football field but, more importantly providing a focus and outlet for young people of all abilities.

Wallsend Boys' Club is a fine example of grass roots community enterprise that harnesses the enthusiasm of our young people and channels it positively, to create a proud institution that is recognised as a prodigious factory line of talent. We as a borough are proud of their achievements and we believe Wallsend Boys' Club are an example to us all. Many of the people involved are volunteers, who give up their time freely and willingly, to put something back into their community and we as a borough, are proud to have played a small part in bringing the Boys' club football teams back to Wallsend and the borough". The motion added "Freedom of the borough is only a small gesture, but we believe it is right to honour the club, as it is rightly seen as part of the fabric of our borough."

The year 2007 was a golden year for the club in other ways. For the first time in their history they were given the opportunity, which was eagerly accepted, to develop their own pitches and changing facilities. This came again with the support of North Tyneside Council and saw the Club begin to develop a £1.4 million complex of seven football pitches, a multi-use games area, changing rooms and car parking facilities at

John Harrison.

Jim Allan.

Rheydt Avenue in Wallsend. These were eventually opened officially in June 2011.

It would be very easy for the connection between Swan Hunters and Wallsend Boys' Club, and the stories of the early history of the club with the pantomimes and other activities no longer fashionable, to slip out of everyone's memory as the years go by. Particularly since in 2006 Swan Hunter's shut it's doors for the last time. To the great delight of the two club stalwarts who had researched and rediscovered this history a grant from the Heritage Lottery Fund announced in February 2011 made that loss of memory less likely.

Vince Carrick and Michael McGill's labour of love was rewarded with a grant of £36,000 from the Fund. This would not only finance the publication of a book (the very one you are reading!) but also the setting up of an educational package through which school pupils will learn about the history of the club

and be able to share in the memories of the older generations. Two of the club's more famous former members spoke of the value they felt this project would have. Alan Shearer said: "I think it is fantastic that this history is going to be recorded. There will be enormous interest in how this club has played such a valuable role in the lives of so many Tyneside youngsters, while producing so many quality footballers."

Michael Carrick also added: "I started going to the club when I was five. The club is doing great work regarding the positive futures of young people".

Just when it seemed that things could not get much better, disaster struck however. In high winds in January 2012 an end wall of the building on Station Road was blown inwards onto the Astro-turf pitch. Luckily this happened at night when the club was empty so no-one was hurt.

However, the effects of the damage led to the whole club house being declared unsafe for future use and in February demolition took place.

What happened next to Wallsend Boys' Club?

Well as you will have gathered this is certainly not the end of the story or in any sense a 'final word'. But the sequel belongs to the next ' History of Wallsend Boys' Club'.

Founder members Fred Tate, Jack Carruthers, Jimmy McBlain and Jack Scott opening the new pitches.

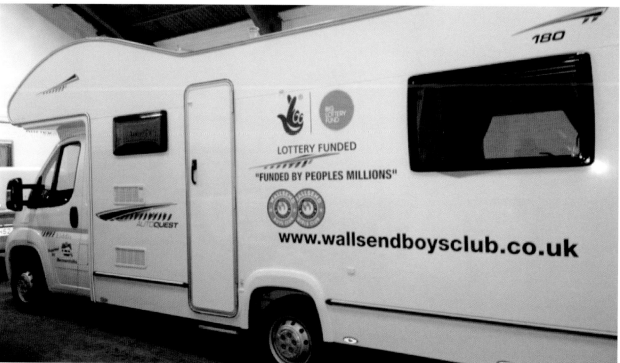

Wallsend Boys' Club Members Who Have Gone On To Play Professional Football

Paul Baker

Steve Baker

Peter Beardsley

Ian Bogie

David Borley

Michael Bridges

James Brown

Steve Bruce

David Bukowski

Adam Campbell

Michael Carrick

Phil Cavener

Vince Chapman

Lee Clark

Tony Dinning

Christie Elliott

Robbie Elliott

Nicky Evans

Graham Fenton

Thomas Flynn

Fraser Forster

Damon Gray

Ray Hankin

Chris Hedworth

Rob Hindmarch

Neil Hooks

Lewis Horner

Shaun Hutchinson

Russell Irving

Clark Keltie

Brian Laws

Gary Leonard

Keith Lockhart

Anthony Lormor

Shaun Lowther

Paul Malcolm

Mark Maley

Kevin McDonald

Neil McDonald

Kevin McGarrigle

Marc Nash

Lee Novak

Derrick Parker

Ben Pringle

Phil Ray

Barry Richardson

David Robinson

David Roche

Tony Sealy

Alan Shearer

Kevin Smith

Eric Steele

Paul Stephenson

Mick Tait

Paul Tait

Jeff Tate

Dan Taylor

Les Taylor

Steven Taylor

Alan Thompson

Alan Waddle

Dean Walker

Barrie Wardrobe

Mick Wardrobe

Ian Watson

John Watson

Steve Watson

Tommy Widdrington

Billy Wright

Jeff Wrightson

To be continued…

Paul Baker

Southampton
Blyth Spartans

Ian Bogie

Newcastle United
Preston North End
Millwall
Leyton Orient
Port Vale
Kidderminster

Michael Bridges

Sunderland
Leeds United
Newcastle United
Bolton Wanderers
Bristol City
Carlisle United
Hull City

Steve Bruce

Norwich City
Manchester United
Birmingham City

Peter Beardsley

Carlisle United
Vancouver
Whitecaps
Newcastle United
Liverpool
Everton
Newcastle United
ENGLAND

Michael Carrick

West Ham United
Tottenham Hotspur
Manchester United
ENGLAND

Phil Cavener

Burnley
Bradford City
Gillingham
Northampton
Town
Peterborough
United
Kettering Town

Lee Clark

Newcastle United
Sunderland
Fulham
Newcastle United

Tony Dinning

Newcastle United
Stockport County
Wolves
Wigan Athletic
Stoke City
Walsall
Blackpool
Ipswich Town
Bristol City
Port Vale

Robbie Elliott

Newcastle United
Bolton Wanderers
Sunderland
Leeds United

Graham Fenton

Aston Villa
West Bromwich
Albion
Blackburn Rovers
Leicester City

Ray Hankin

Burnley
Leeds United

Chris Hedworth

Newcastle United
Barnsley
Halifax
Blackpool

Rob Hindmarch
(R.I.P.)

Sunderland
Derby County

Russell Irving

Ipswich Town
Cardiff City
Colchester

Brian Laws

Burnley
Huddersfield Town
Middlesbrough
Nottingham Forest
Darlington
Grimsby Town
Scunthorpe United

Gary Leonard

West Bromwich
Albion
Shrewsbury
Bury
Hereford
Stockport

Anthony Lormor

Newcastle United
Chesterfield
Notts County
Preston
Mansfield
Hartlepool United

Paul Malcolm

Newcastle United
Shrewsbury Town
Barnsley
Doncaster Rovers

Kevin McDonald

Hibernian

Neil McDonald

Newcastle United
Everton
Oldham
Preston
Bolton Wanderers

Marc Nash

Hartlepool United

Phil Ray

West Bromwich
Albion
Plymouth Argyle

David Robinson

Newcastle United
Reading
Peterborough United
Blackpool
Cambridge United

Tony Sealy

Southampton
Crystal Palace
Queens Park Rangers
Fulham
Leicester City
Bournemouth
Sporting Lisbon
Bristol Rovers
Brentford
Hong Kong FC

Alan Shearer

Southampton
Blackburn Rovers
Newcastle United
ENGLAND

Eric Steele

Newcastle United
Peterborough United
Brighton
Watford
Derby County
Aston Villa

Paul Stephenson

Newcastle United
Millwall
Brentford
York City
Hartlepool United

Mick Tait

Hull City
Portsmouth
Reading
Hartlepool United
Darlington

Jeff Tate

Burnley

Steven Taylor

Newcastle United
ENGLAND
under 21's

Alan Thompson

Newcastle United
Bolton Wanderers
Aston Villa
Celtic
Leeds United
ENGLAND

John Watson

Newcastle United
Scunthorpe United

Steve Watson

Newcastle United
Aston Villa
Everton
West Bromwich
Albion

Tommy Widdrington

Southampton
Wigan
Grimsby
Port Vale
Hartlepool
Macclesfield

Jeff Wrightson

Newcastle United
Preston North End

Barrie Wardrobe

Sunderland
St Mirren
Hartlepool

Steve Baker
Southampton

David Bukowski
Northampton Town

Keith Lockhart
Cambridge United

Shaun Lowther
Vancouver Whitecaps
CANADA

Kevin McGarrigle
Brighton

Derrick Parker
Burnley
Oldham Athletic
Rochdale

David Roche
Newcastle United

Kevin Smith
Cambridge United
Exeter
Torquay

Les Taylor
Oxford United

Alan Waddle
Liverpool

Dean Walker
Burnley
Barnsley
Scunthorpe

Mick Wardrobe
Burnley
Stockport County
Macclesfield

Ian Watson
Sunderland
Newport County

Billy Wright
NEW ZEALAND

Where are they now?

First Boys' Club first team under 18's.

TBC   Eric Lee   TBC   Rog Walters   Ian Riccalton   Frank Blane
Derek Wells   TBC   Alan Dodds   TBC   TBC

Rog Walters   John Graham   TBC   TBC   TBC   George McBlain
Alan Dodds   TBC   TBC   Ian Rickleton   TBC

TBC   TBC   Shaun Whelan   TBC   Robbin Batey   Bruce Ward   Duncan Bruce
Paul Tait   Dave Hill   David Atkinson   Michael Walker   Tony Bradley   Norman Kelly

Kevin Lowery   Billy Rogers   Derek Homer   Tim M   Taylor Holmes   Phil Redford   TBC
TBC   Joe Rice   John Weatherit   Russel Abbot   John Bolton   TBC

TBC   TBC   Tim M   Phil Rowland   TBC   Thompson
TBC   TBC   Dave Nichol   Terry Pigg   TBC   John Hailes

Paul TBC   TBC   Vince Stubbs   Dave McParland   Dave McDonald   Rob White   TBC
Alan Lodge   Tim Hutchinson   Cliff Thompson   TBC   TBC   TBC

Martin Lee - To Dad, Merry Christmas! Love Robyn, Dan, Becca & Dan. Xxxxx

Linda Gibson - Many familiar faces from days gone by

Colin Cunningham - Happy xmas dad from richie

George Urwin - Happy Christmas - Love, Graeme & Linsey Xxx

Jack Lucy - To Grandad Jack, love Seb xx

Stewart Brockman

Alan Wilson - Merry Christmas 2013 to a Wallsend old boy

Daddy - Looking forward to our great footballing times. Love Matthew

to David Jonathan - With love from mum xxx

Ken Jackson - Happy Christmas 2013 xxx

Dad - Merry Christmas, hope you enjoy the book! Love from Alec

Fiona Fearns

To Jonathan - Happy Christmas from Helen and Mick

Bob Hall - To the Glory Days! Love Dan & Nadia - Christmas 2013

Dennis Crossley - To Den, Merry Christmas.... Love Kath X x X x

Andrew Tierney

Bob Wilson - What if?

Tom Rantoul - Tom Rantoul - great memories of playing for WBC 1982-1988!

Grandad - Merry Christmas, grandad! Love Jack x

Dad - Merry Christmas!

Dad - There's no mention of our famous 0-0 at 5 a side. Alan

Samuel Warren - Merry Xmas Samuel, all our love Mam and Dad !

Joseph Lackenby - Good luck with your football Joseph Love Mam n Dad

William Manning - Happy Christmas 2013, All my love, Paula

Chris Coulthard - Many thanks to Pete and the Coaches, so many owe you so much

Eric Steele - Look back with fondness and pride... With love, Elaine xxx

Keith Herron - Hope you enjoy the read - Happy Christmas

Ken - Merry Christmas

David Wilkinson - Working Class Footballing History. Enjoy!

Martin barrett - Martin Barrett - Wallsend Rovers 1995 - 1998

David Robinson - A special part of your history too - Love Julie & Katie xx

Arthur Graham - Medal-winning Wallsend Boy, 1949-50

Brian Hordon - Best goalie this side of the Tyne!

Daniel Gardner - A History of Wallsend Boys Club

Gail Wray - Happy christmas Gail, love from Danny & Joseph xxx

Pops - Merry Christmas Pops from Milla and JoJo xx

George Croudace - Happy Christmas Da, love you loads. Nik

Dad - Merry Xmas Love From Graeme, Michelle, Daniel, Sam & Luke

John Forrest - Coach for over 14 yrs at WBC - enjoyed every minute

Tom Watson - Keep the conveyor belt going

Gordon Edward Roll - Happy Christmas 2013 - all the best dad. X

Gary O'Connor - Great memories of shin pads, socks and smiles!!! Love Sis X

Robert Elwell - Merry Xmas Dad Hope you enjoy the read! X

Eric Hately - Merry Christmas 2013

John Naylor - Happy Birthday 2013

Andrew - Merry Christmas - hope you enjoy this book

Alan Coulson - All the best, Phil & Lesley

David Taylor - You played your part. So proud of you Boy...Luv Ya Dad x

Dominic Riley - History which you were part of.

Lee Hall

Dad - Happy Christmas and happy reading

Billy Sloan - Player of the Year 1970/71

Sandra McGill - For being patient for 10 years while I co-wrote the book

Lucas McGill - To a grandson in a million from Sandra and Michael McGill

Darren Thompson - Come on WHITES let's go - HAPPY DAYS

David Samuel Airey - Merry First Family Christmas 2013, Love always, Julia x

Raymond Oliver - A friend who eagerly awaited this book to which he added to.

Gary Larkin - All the greats are from Wallsend!
Love from the wifey xxx

Kevin Vale - To Grandpa - lots of happy football
memories!

Ryan Kendall - Where it all started when you were
5 years old xxxx

Alan Thompson - Merry Christmas Dad!

Neil Jensen - Keeping the WBC dream alive
in Hong Kong

Derek Henderson

Paul Rogers

Greg Young - Loyal member of Bob Sloane's army

Steven Young - Under 16 Player of the Year 1995-96

Nicholas bone - Holy Cross 1985 5-a-side the start of
it all

Tony Annan - Old Boy 1984-1989. Great days.

Ian Cusack - Wallsend Boys Club & UCU; True
Socialism in North Tyneside

Jonny Forrest - 2000-12 great teams, great
friendships, great club!

Bill Lisgo - Hope this holds happy memories -
Love from Linda and Dave

Brandon Robson - Merry Christmas Brandon
Love from Mam and Dad 2013

Neil Freestone - Merry Christmas Granda Love from
Brandon, Logan, Molly and Daisy 2013

Grandad - Lots of love Alfie xxx

Michael Robson - Merry Christmas Granda Love from
Brandon, Logan, Molly and Daisy 2013

Dad - Lots of love Alfie xxx

Graeme Carrick - To Graeme, Your a Son to be Proud
of. Love always from Dad x

Michael Carrick - To Michael, A Son to be Proud of.
Love always from Dad x

Miss Edith Gill - Merry Christmas from David

Vince Carrick - To Vince, Well done! It's only taken
10 years hard work xx

Paul Devine - You still owe me your subs money from
Wed 28th Sep 1977!!

Nigel Devine - Hope you enjoy kid, all the best your
fav bro Mark

Michael McDonald - This should bring back some
happy memories kid

Shaun McGill - We are very proud of you love for
eternity from Mam and Dad

Adam McGill - We are very proud of you love for
eternity from Mam and Dad

Mam and Dad - Thanks for everything

Anthony Thompson - To Dad, lots of love Lol,
Bob and DJ xx

Ruth Vale - Chris Vale; WBC Player of the Year 1981
and 1983

Ruth Vale - Chris Vale; WBC Player of the Year 1981
and 1983

Chris - Merry Christmas 2013 - from North East to
North West

Andy Taylor - Merry Christmas 2013 Andy
from Nick x

Kevin Dodds - The Good Old Times. Enjoy. X

John Pringle - To our favourite Geordie love
Laura & Geoff xx

Dad - Happy Christmas 2013 xxx

Dad - Merry Christmas 2015

Andy Farrell

Michael Farrell

Alan Sayers

Dad - Hope you enjoy reading all about the club.
Love you Kerry x

Alan Burgess - Merry Christmas from all the Todds

Mick Todd - Biggest sports fan ever

Keith Gray - Hope this brings back some memories!

Bill Heslop - Happy reading!

Andrew Bowman - Happy Christmas from Mam and
Kevin xx

Steven Revell - Happy Christmas

Mark Leighton - Great memories of the Boyza

Phil White - Thanks to Peter Kirkley and the WBC,
a big part of my life.

Mr Robert Murray - Happy christmas lots of love
Shirley and Glyn xx

Paul Davies - Memories of a good time in your life –
A. H. Davies.

The Boys of '69 who had Willington Quay & Howdon
BC and WBC at heart. Bill Lisgo

Stella Michaela Megan Bryony Siobhan & Niamh
thanks for indulging my time at WBC

For all the Conway family – still going strong – Mr M

In memory of Micky Joyce and Johnny Morris – Rest
in Peace lads – John Mason

Dennis Dale – 29/09/1934 to 03/09/2008. You would
have loved Bigges Main!

I came, I saw, I settled down! Hadrian, Emperor of
Rome (AD 127)

Thanks and acknowledgements:

The authors wish to thank the following people for their help, contributions and shared memories:

Ray "Pang" Oliver
Jack Carruthers
Jimmy McBlain
Bill Watson
Jack Scott
Fred "Spud" Tate
Eddie "Bunty" Young
Norman Livingstone
Bob Corkhill
Tony Corkhill
John McNally
Alan Heward
Joyce Herdman
Ronnie Lane
John McGuinness
Terry Sweeney
John Gibson (of the Chronicle)
The Mag
True Faith
nufc.com
The Back Page
Newcastle United Supporters Trust
Chris Mort (Freshfields)

We also acknowledge the following publications for their articles on the Boys' Club over the years, which helped us piece together the story:

Newcastle Evening Chronicle
The Journal
Herald & Post
Wallsend News
Daily Mail
Mail on Sunday magazine 'Night & Day'
Sunday Post
Daily Express
Sunday Sun
The Football Pink
Wallsend News Guardian
Ordnance Survey
North Shields Library
Watford F.C.
Tyne and Wear Archive services
North Tyneside Libraries

Reference is also made to the History of the Parish of Wallsend, written in 1923 by William Richardson and reprinted by Newcastle and North Tyneside Libraries.

Our thanks go to the Heritage Lottery Fund for their financial support.

PRINTING • PACKAGING • DIRECT MAIL

www.potts.co.uk

Thank you to Potts Print (UK)
for their co-operation in the printing of this book

FSC
MIX
Paper
FSC® C019788

WORLD
LAND
TRUST™

www.carbonbalancedpaper.com
Potts Print (UK) Reg. No. 2105

This is a carbon balanced publication. The carbon impact of this printed item
has been estimated and offset through the conservation of endangered tropical
rainforest. Potts Print (UK): The first Carbon Balanced printing company in the
North of England. Find out more at www.potts.co.uk/greenprint